We All Wore Blue

We All Wore Blue

Muriel Gane Pushman

Robson Books

First published in Great Britain in 1989 by Robson Books Ltd,
Bolsover House, 5–6 Clipstone Street, London W1P 7EB

Copyright © 1989 The Pickering Press

British Library Cataloguing in Publication Data

Pushman, Muriel Gane, 1921 –
  We all wore blue: Funny, romantic and moving – a
  young girl's adventures in the wartime WAAF.
  1. Great Britain. Royal Air Force. Women's Auxiliary
  Air Force – Biographies
  I. Title
  3584'4'1348'0924

ISBN 0 86051 588 5

Printed in Great Britain by St Edmundsbury Press Ltd
Bury St Edmunds, Suffolk.

I DEDICATE this, my posy of wartime memories, to my grandchildren and the many W.A.A.F. friends whom I gathered along the way.

Contents

Foreword

WORLD WAR II, following the pattern of World War I,
saw a long stride forward in the emancipation of
women, the development of their activities, and the appre-
ciation of their capabilities. Until this century, with rare
exceptions, the role of women in war was passive: they
bade farewell to the departing warriors, took care of the
families, wept for the fallen, and occasionally and usually
unhappily found themselves among the prizes of war. War
was for professional soldiers and sailors, supplemented by
enthusiastic amateurs strictly from the male population.

In the twentieth century, the scope and spread of wars
widened dramatically. They were fought among entire na-
tions and included—were compelled to include—women.
Their first role was as nurses and sisters of mercy; then in
industry; finally in uniform, although only in the Soviet
Union as actual combatants. Muriel Gane, a pretty, sheltered, unsophisticated girl of eighteen from a close and
happy English middle-class family, found herself swept up
in this tide of events.

As she records, the whole mood of the country and its
people changed as they went to war. She herself was
among the earlier volunteers, choosing the Women's Royal
Air Force, as she frankly admits, largely because the
colour of the uniform suited her. It is the frankness and
naturalness of her writing that are among the chief attrac-
tions of this book. She was obviously a success in her
chosen vocation, was commissioned as an officer, and
learnt to lead as well as to serve. She does not exaggerate

her achievements or overdramatize her experiences. Hers is the story of an attractive young woman, much sought after by her male comrades but also making many friends among the female.

Hers is indeed a story of comradeship, of novel experience, of courage and determination, told with modesty, humour, and great charm. It should appeal not only to her own generation but also to the wide reading public who are interested in a history which maintains a light personal touch throughout.

AIR CHIEF MARSHAL
SIR CHRISTOPHER FOXLEY-NORRIS
GCB, DSO, OBE, RAF RET'D.
CHAIRMAN, THE BATTLE OF BRITAIN FIGHTER ASSOCIATIOON

Acknowledgments

I WOULD LIKE to thank my family for their support in this project, especially my husband, George, whose unflagging enthusiasm and optimism sustained me throughout. The effort would not have been possible without Winifred Denny, my friend who helped fuse these tales into a book. My thanks go also to Lavinia Warner for providing needed encouragement, and to all my friends who read my stories and enjoyed them. I am indebted to my publisher, June Pimm; Charity Johnson, Editor-in-Chief at The Pickering Press; and J. Kendall Pepper, for all their work in shaping the manuscript.

1939-1941

We Go to War

I TURNED eighteen that summer of 1939. It had been a glorious August, with warm, balmy days that created a seductive serenity as we slipped toward September. Beneath the surface there was uneasiness and fear. It was obvious that war was imminent, but how it would appear and how it would alter our lives, we could only imagine. Most of us moved into that last summer of peace in a hedonistic spirit of taking pleasure while it was still to be found.

It was 11 a.m on September 3rd, and we were at breakfast when my father turned on the wireless. In the quiet of the room, the box crackled intrusively like noisy sweet papers in the cinema, then above the static we heard the voice of the Prime Minister, Neville Chamberlain. I do not remember everything he said, only the terrible clarity of the announcement, "This country is now in a state of war with Germany."

It was difficult to sort out my emotions. There was a falling away sensation in my stomach, and the classic shiver up my spine; but there was also a rather guilty sense of excitement, as though some rare and splendid adventure was waiting in the wings, and I was centre stage.

My father set out to reassure us. He said there was no cause for immediate alarm; that it would take considerable time to set the wheels of war in action, and this would give Britain time to organize. My mother said she hoped he was right, but stated that she felt the Germans were more than prepared.

My own mind had left the room and gone to Dover Beach, where I imagined the Germans landing that very minute, stumbling over bathing tents and deck chairs, on their way to take over my England. There flashed onto my inner eye the horrific newsreels I had seen of Nazis rounding up Jews in the German cities. Now we were at war with such people. The chill of fear returned. Could things like that happen here?

The next day, my father announced his decision to enlist. He felt that there would be jobs going, particularly for those who had been in the last war. My mother said nothing, but I knew what she was thinking. She had confided in me not long before that if war came, she would love to go back into nursing. She had been a nursing sister in World War I, and perhaps her desire to return to her profession was a way of establishing her own identity once more. Women like my mother did not plant feminist flags nor hurl challenges. So if my father wished to go, it was clear she would have to stay. It was necessary for someone to keep the estate going and look after the family. She may have felt a little wistful but by no means martyred. I suppose women all over the country were accepting similar choiceless decisions, and slipping into the slots where they would be most productive.

My father was a solicitor and had a highly developed sense of moral principle. He was unbending in the standard of behavior he set for himself, and hoped his children would follow his lead. However, he had a nice sense of humour as well as a first-rate mind, and to me he was an immeasurably comforting sort of person. I adored him, and was his shadow. Somewhere in the family album, there is a picture of me in the obligatory Christopher Robin garb of the twenties' child, standing just behind my father and unconsciously aping his stance.

My mother was a Canadian from the small town of Bowmanville, Ontario. She was, in the admittedly biased opinion of her children, not only the best mother in the world, but also the core of our household. She provided a happy balance in the family, bringing a kind of transatlantic freshness into our lives that nicely counteracted any tendency we might have had toward county stuffiness. She had a busy life with many responsibilities, as my sister Audrey was the victim of a rare, unidentifiable condition that was turning her into an invalid at thirteen; and in 1939 Diana, my maddening, adorable, baby sister, was only five years old.

In addition to my parents and sisters, the family unit had been extended to include my remarkable and cherished paternal grandmother. A special, self-contained flat had been arranged for her in one wing of the house, and here she held court with her maid, Cynthia, in attendance. Not strictly family, although it never occurred to us to think of them as anything else, were Nellie, our cook, and her sister, Flo, who was our nanny.

Our family lived at Warren Farm House, which lay in a hundred and eighty acres of wood and field in the broad sweep of the Surrey Downs, just outside Guildford. It was reputed to have been an inn in Chaucer's time, when pilgrims walked from Winchester to Canterbury to pay homage at Thomas à Becket's shrine. It had been our home since 1934, when my father acquired it to house his growing family; to keep horses; and simply because he fell in love with it. Although his office was in The Temple, he gladly made the journey into the City each day for the sheer joy of coming home to such a refuge each night.

We children were brought up with tremendous care, and a great deal of love. As very little children we were always under the watchful eye of Nanny, in the nursery or on our daily walk. It was a pattern that never changed, and perhaps for that very reason it added to our already firmly rooted sense of security. Even the early packing off to boarding school was not regarded as any type of banishment. It was part of the established order of things, and we were expected to have the backbone to gain from the good in the system, and to learn to overcome any of the negative aspects.

Although Nanny, in particular, was a firm disciplinarian, and allowed no disrespect to man nor beast, our life style as children was, nonetheless, fairly relaxed. We had a wonderful menagerie of horses, ponies, dogs, and cats, and on our early morning rides we were always accompanied by a cavalcade of dogs, trailing along after us as far as their physical limitations would allow. Inside, cats were perennially curled in baskets, and our assortment of dogs lolled beside the fireplace. There was such a tranquil pattern to our existence that the swift changes brought about by the declaration of war seemed doubly violent.

Within a week, I am sure my mother's wish for the comparative calm of life as a nursing sister must have turned into a passionate prayer. A day or two after the war had begun, a billeting officer marched down the long drive to our front door and almost immediately, it seemed to us, conjured up a whole batch of new residents for Warren Farm House.

First to arrive were a pair of seven-year-old cockneys, John and Helen, freckle-faced, street-wise, and country-ignorant. Their total disregard for the refinements of living was a shock to Nanny, but their natural ebullience and brash charm soon had her as devoted to them as she was to Diana.

They were followed by a medical student called Tony Howarth, who had the good taste to be what I then considered "divinely good-looking." He came to us when part of St. Thomas' Hospital Medical School was tranferred from London to Guildford. He did not, however, come empty-handed, but arrived leading a grey mare, none too originally dubbed Silver, and asked my mother if she could board her. Mother, always a pushover for a handsome young man, agreed, and Silver went off to join Sally, Stjarni, our Icelandic pony, and the others in the already bulging stables. Two nurses arrived a few days later, and finally, a very pukkha colonel and his wife.

All these arrivals fell to my mother to organize, with help from Nellie and Nanny. The logistics were horrendous:

beds were dug out of the attic; there was a vast re-arrange-
ment of sleeping quarters; linen and blankets were bor-
rowed from the Red Cross; and every square inch of space
was utilized. Rationing was already in effect, and my father, always the soul of honour, hinted darkly at what
would befall any member of his family caught bending the
rules. It was here that Nellie came into her own. In the
kitchen, she was inventive, tireless, and frugal, and somehow managed, like Jesus, to make the rations for five
stretch to feed five hundred.

It was strange how the mood of Britain changed instantly once war was declared. Everyone wanted in some
way to be involved in the effort. My father had his wish,
and was accepted into the Army and found himself working at the War Office, where he had great pleasure in telling everybody that he was an inmate at Wormwood
Scrubbs prison: his office was one of many small cells.

The day the news of his acceptance arrived, I was taken
aback to hear my dignified parent whooping like a school-
boy. He immediately hared up to the attic to try to find his
World War I Sam Brown, and emerged some time later in
clouds of dust and flights of moths, but clutching his
treasure triumphantly. He was even more chuffed to find it
still fitted him some twenty years on.

We, the family, had our lives turned upside down. No
longer could we have our own bedrooms; our serene and
secluded home had overnight become like Waterloo Station. There was bustle everywhere, and a great shortage of
chairs to sit on. In fact, our own private invasion had
taken place, and secretly we were enjoying the new and
exciting life at Warren Farm House.

In the meantime, the sleepy little market town of Guildford was suddenly alive and teeming with strangers, and
in every village and hamlet in the county, people were
suddenly finding themselves decked out in old or new
uniforms. Familiar neighbours in unfamiliar military attire appeared looking faintly self-conscious.

I remember seeing old Mr. Brown from further up the

road in his Air Raid Warden outfit. For years he had barely been able to hobble about due to severe arthritis, but the uniform had somehow stiffened both his resolve and his spine, and now here he was striding along like a sergeant-major on parade. A doddery "Dad's Army" Home Guard sprang up; the Women's Institute turned its attention from flower shows to the Red Cross; and confused children were taken from the threatened cities to the comparative safety of the country. We were a nation shaking ourselves awake to an overpowering reality.

I was too young to think of what was happening in large cosmic terms, but in retrospect I am convinced that no one I knew ever really conceived the possibility of ultimate defeat. The general mood seemed to be summed up by one of the local farmhands: "I reckon it's going to be a bit of a muck up, but no Jerry is ever going to put his great thumping jackboot on Surrey soil, not while Sam Collins is about."

So, armed with a belief in the justice of their cause, faith in their leaders, and love of their land, the people of Britain went to war.

Deciding on Blue

U NKNOWN to anyone, I, too, was determined to partici-
pate in the war effort by joining one of the women's
services, but I realized that the thought was not necessar-
ily going to be mother to the deed. I was convinced my parents would have a full-scale fit. To them, I was still a child
to be protected and sheltered against a world I was as yet
too inexperienced to enter.

I would like to think now that I wanted so desperately to
enlist out of unalloyed patriotism, but I was a typical teen-
ager, female to the core. The thought of cutting a dashing
figure in a chic uniform had an irresistible appeal. I used
to lie in bed at night and ponder which one of the three
uniforms would suit me best. Well, actually, it was two.
The Auxiliary Territorial Service was out; I could not stand
the thought of khaki. On the other hand, the Women's
Royal Naval Service were given black silk stockings, a plus
in any woman's war. No, I thought, it has to be the
Women's Auxiliary Air Force. In life, I reasoned, one has
be fair to oneself and try to nurture one's natural assets.
As a blue-eyed blonde, I had always been besotted with
blue. It was my colour, and so my conscience, my ego, and
I met in agreement and the W.A.A.F. was elected.

The decision made, I cooked up some excuse to go to
London, headed for the W.A.A.F. Recruiting Office, and
offered my services. My guilt was enormous, but my excitement even more so.

The next few weeks were an agony. I was dying to tell
someone what I had done, but did not dare. I was so afraid

that if my father found out, he might try to stop the whole thing. I haunted the letter box, convinced that the Air Force had lost my application; rejected me; forgotten me; anything but accepted me. It was New Year's Eve when the Air Ministry envelope finally arrived. I took it up, unseen, to my bedroom. Emotionally, I was ready to self-destruct, and kept fumbling with the wretched thing before I could open it.

"The Air Ministry is pleased to inform . . . ." It was all I needed to know—I was in! My heart sang, but as I read on I saw that I had to report at Bush House, the Air Ministry headquarters in London, on Monday, January 6th, at 12 noon. Today was December 31st, which gave me only one week to prepare myself, and more importantly my parents, for the departure of their fledgling.

I dreaded the thought of telling them. Opportunities came and went, and I failed to find an appropriate time. My father's time at home was so limited, and his moments of relaxation so rare that I hated to spoil them. My mother, on the other hand, never seemed to have a second to sit down, let alone relax. I knew I could not put it off, time being what it was, so finally after dinner, I approached the drawing room where my parents were having their coffee by the fire. I drew a deep breath, turned the handle, and went in.

They looked up unaware, poor dears, that a momentous announcement was about to be made. My resolution wavered. Maybe I should just sit down, have a coffee, and tell them tomorrow. No, I thought grimly, dredging up the Bard: "If it were done . . . then 'twere well it were done quickly."

As the moment approached, I took a deep breath: "I've got some important news for you two." I felt I was going to choke. My father looked up and I could hear myself talking with the sensation of total detachment from the voice within me. It was a strong voice, no longer a little girl's; a voice with a purpose. Looking down at the floor, I went on without interruption until I had said all that I wanted to say.

Nobody spoke. The air was electric, the only sound being the rhythmic breathing of the dogs sprawled in front of the fire. Oh to hell, I thought, with this damned war and what it is doing to our family. The suspense was awful and I was close to tears.

Finally, I raised my eyes and looked first at my father and then at my mother. To my utter amazement, they were both smiling. My father rose from his chair and came toward me with outstretched arms. In a second I was in them, finding the unfailing source of security and comfort. My mother stood up and joined us, and for a few moments we stood together without speaking.

It all seemed somehow quite natural, although we were not a particularly demonstrative family. I cherished the closeness of the moment and the warmth of that protective circle, yet paradoxically, I felt, for the first time in my life, separate and apart. My parents were still as dear to me as I to them, but I was now an individual entity with decisions to reach and mistakes to make. As of that evening, I had earned the right to find my way alone into the undiscovered land of my own future.

* * *

My father was the first one to break the mood. With a suspicious clearing of the throat, he announced that with a new year and a daughter both about to be launched, the occasion called for nothing less than the best bubbly in the house. The champagne was at once produced and the rest of the household was summoned to hear the news.

They all poured in: my sisters, my grandmother and her maid, Cynthia, Nanny and Nellie; even our Cowman, Bill, and his wife, whom we all affectionately called Mrs. Bill, rushed over from their cottage on the other side of the farm yard. In addition to the normal residents, the newcomers also filtered in, and the whole thing turned into a proper party. I was toasted, wished well, hugged, and advised. Advice, I was to learn in the days that followed, was unavoidable. I had to be patient with the "little chats" given in private by both my parents, who had fears for what they insisted on calling my "well being." True to their upbringing and generation, they could not bring themselves to discuss sex as such, so they contented themselves with oblique references to men, drink, and "crafty wiles." Even then, they did not define "crafty wiles," but communicated through polite innuendoes, lots of raising of eyebrows and nods of heads, all of which left me as ignorant as before all these little chats took place.

I was amused that my parents should be so concerned about instructing me in the ways of the wicked world, as I felt I knew all about love, being madly attached to Donald, the son of one of our neighbours.

It seemed to me there had never been a time when Donald had not been there. He was two years older than I, and had been my constant companion whenever we were both home from school. We had shared childhood secrets and adolescent fears, he had nicknamed me "Moo," and I loved him incredibly. It was a happy time to be young; we played tennis, went riding, and attended well-chaperoned dances. In our private moments, we had a tender and tentative relationship, governed by the moral code of the day.

Now, in the flurry of departure, I felt only an unreasonable sense of resentment that Donald was not around to share the excitement of my going. He had qualified as a solicitor just after the declaration of war, promptly joined the Navy, and was posted almost immediately. Having a fairly developed sense of the dramatic, I imagined a touching farewell scene with Donald, pale and devastated, and me, looking brave, noble and, of course, ravishingly beautiful. It was in every respect a thoroughly satisfying little scenario, and it was small wonder I felt cheated.

Finally, it was my last night at home. I looked around my room: at my pretty, four-poster bed, the covers turned down invitingly, and nightgown in place on the pillow. I saw the comforting bulge of the hot water bottle Nanny had put there, and tears pricked my eyes. This had been my life, and I had taken it all for granted. Now I was leaving it, and here I was, at the last moment, in a wild ambivalence of emotions, with only one absolute certainty. I was scared to death.

The next morning came with the inevitability of a dawn execution. It seemed to me the entire county was down at the railway station to see me off, and I felt the way I used to when going back to boarding school. There was a nasty, sick feeling in the pit of my stomach, my eyes smarted, and my throat felt dry. "Please, God," I prayed, "let the train hurry up, let me get the farewells over, oh please let it come before I start to cry."

It snaked in very, very slowly, and I climbed aboard with almost indecent haste. I leant out the window to make my last farewells and I could feel warm tears trickling down my cheeks. I waved and waved until the people, who up until now had been my whole life, became lost in the landscape like specks in the desert. The carriage was empty except for an elderly gentleman in the far corner, who seemed totally oblivious to the magnitude of the moment. I huddled into the opposite corner, feeling vulnerable and utterly alone.

Upon arriving at the Air Ministry, I found the whole place buzzing with activity. I dodged past two R.A.F. lorries, already loaded with meagre bits of luggage brought in by the new recruits. Inside, the whole place seemed full of bustling people, snapping out orders and moving about purposefully. By contrast, the collection of apprehensive females in the corner, of which I would soon be one, appeared awkward and in the way. They looked pretty wretched, and I wondered how many were having second thoughts. I banished my own, with a bracing talk from my "inner friend," an imaginary companion I had created for comfort when I first went away to school. The gist of our unilateral conversation was to pull myself together, that everyone else was in the same boat, and for heaven's sake to stop snivelling.

To divert myself I looked around at the girls who were to be my companions for the next six weeks. My initial reaction was that they were a pretty mixed bunch. My casual surveillance stopped suddenly at one recruit. It was not just because of her appearance— although that was certainly arresting enough— it was her voice, which she was now using to telling effect. The old simile of foghorn is the only one adequate to describe its blasting force; it was also pure cockney and spiced with the richness of the dockland vernacular. She was about thirty, very fat, and seemed to be made of rolls, rather like the Michelin tyre man, with a halo of brightly dyed hair, orange like the rising sun.

I was transfixed and knew I was staring at her in the rudest possible way. I was saved from what might have been a very colourful ticking off by hearing my name called out. I leapt as though I had been stabbed. The R.A.F. sergeant looked toward me, and I relaxed with gratitude as he gave me a big, kind smile. He is human, at least, I thought. He motioned me forward.

"When I call out your name tomorrow, Miss, I shall expect you to say, loud and clear, 'Yes, Sergeant.'"

I nodded meekly and felt myself turning a brilliant shade of pink. I had always hated my propensity for blushing, and only wished I could grow out of it. The sergeant ticked off my name, and told me to get into the lorry. Here at least I was grateful for my long legs. Some of the shorter girls had a terrible time trying to reach the tail board, and my hennaed friend had to be hoisted up with the aid of three sturdy men.

We were finally all in, and perched nervously on the benches that lined the lorry.

"I wonder where they are taking us," said one of the girls.

"King's Cross Station," replied another, in the sort of voice that implied. "Don't you know *anything.*" I turned to look at the oracle and saw the classic "Bossy Boots" of

every school room. Everything about her seemed aggres-
sive. She was short and stalky, with thick sturdy legs, like
miniature tree trunks, I thought. She was also monumen-
tally plain, which probably accounted for a lot of her asser-
tiveness. While the rest of us sat engrossed in our private,
none-too-happy thoughts, she became increasingly vol-
uble on where we were going, what we could expect when
we got there, and how she would see us all through. After
a while, she of the orange hair, not to be outdone, put her
conversational oar in, and the two of them ground on like a
gramophone record stuck in a groove.

We arrived at King's Cross, which in my depressed state
of mind looked larger, greyer, and more austere than ever.
We boarded a train for Harrogate, and I looked gloomily
out a window already dribbled by rain. It was a miserable
day, and as the train sped northwards, all I was aware of
as I contemplated the sodden fields and leafless trees was
that I was as dreary as the landscape. Would I ever, I
asked myself, be lucky enough to meet a kindred spirit?
Would I have to spend the entire war with this dismal lot?
The thought appalled me, and my wretchedness increased.

By the time we reached Harrogate, the city was in total
darkness. Not only was it January, but blackout regulations were in effect as well. I had never travelled north
before. In fact Oxford, notable in my unacademic young
mind purely for its May Balls, was as far north as I had
ever ventured. All I could think was that if this was The
North, they could keep it. Once again we were herded into
a lorry and driven off into the darkness. We bounced and
bumped along, our destination a mystery. Suddenly the
lorry swung clumsily into a driveway, scattering everyone
hither and thither across the floor.

There was silence; then someone laughed. It was instantly infectious, bursting like a shooting star over the
pile of bodies as each person frantically tried to untangle
herself. When we did finally return to our places on the
narrow benches, it was no longer in stiff, isolated little

units. The laughter had been all that was needed to break the ice of our reserve. I think perhaps we all looked at each other for the first time, not just as a jumble of girls from all walks of life, but as a potential homogeneous whole. I did not know it then, but in the next few years I would learn to live side by side with strangers, gain from them as colleagues, and leave them as friends.

A Bird in Blue

OUR HOME for the next three weeks was to be the Majestic Hotel in Harrogate—a massive Victorian building with large and extremely elegant reception rooms, which were now filled with the Royal Air Force standard furniture and fittings. All the finery of pre-war days had been carefully stowed away in moth balls for the duration of the war. The floors were bare and the walls devoid of pictures, but the carved woodwork and fine ceilings were still there for us to admire.

The place was a-buzz with people in R.A.F. and W.A.A.F. uniforms dashing in every direction, all looking terribly efficient and as if they knew what they were about. We, on the other hand, must have appeared a rather pathetic sight, as we hung about in small groups, uncertain as to what to do or where to go. We were not in doubt for very long: a little knot of non-commissioned officers advanced upon us, smiling their welcome.

"You poor dears," one said, "you all look frozen. We'll organize some supper right away. It's surprising what a cup of hot tea will do to bring warmth back into your bones. Put your coats down on that bench over there and then follow us into the dining hall."

This was more like it, I thought, things are looking up. I began to feel human again, to such an extent that by the time I reached the dining hall, I had made up my mind to work like mad toward getting some N.C.O. stripes. With any luck, I told myself, I might even get a commission.

The dining hall was vast and I joined the very first—but certainly not the last—queue in my life. We were soon to learn that from now on queues were formed for everything, and just like homing pigeons we automatically joined one, sometimes without knowing exactly what we were queuing for!

When my turn came, I was asked if I wished to have tea—with sugar or without. I replied "without," but found upon taking a sip later that it was *loaded* with it, and tasted like treacle! This apparently was a common occurrence, and rather than re-join the queue and go through the motions all over again, one just accepted one's lot, which no doubt was the cause of many a change in tea drinking habits.

For a while, however, I feared that this first supper might also be my last. I had the healthy appetite of a normal teen-ager, but I was bowled over by the mammoth portions being heaped on my plate. A mountain of potatoes was slapped on with a generous hand. Around this, mushy peas swilled like a sea of green paint, underneath which a couple of sausages could be seen peeping out as though gasping for air. Ugh, I thought, I will never get through all this. Surprisingly enough, I did, and what's more, I thoroughly enjoyed it. Listening to the grumbling going on around me, I blessed my years at boarding school. If nothing else, they had taught me to eat what was put in front of me, and without comment.

After this orgy of carbohydrates, we were told to report to the Reception Hall. It was obvious the Air Force was not leaving any margin for error, as a gigantic signboard announced: "New Recruits—Report Here." The new regimentation of our lives began at this desk. A W.A.A.F. sergeant called out our names and divided us into two groups, A and B. These two units were then subdivided into two smaller groups, and bedrooms were allocated. At this stage, of course, names meant nothing, so it was not until everyone staggered off to bed that it was revealed who our roommates were to be for the next three weeks.

Imagine the unpleasant jolt it gave me to discover that of my five roommates, one was the red-haired butterball, aptly called Rosie, and another was Miss Know-It-All. She introduced herself with a pulverizing handshake as Mavis, and somehow managed to suggest that I should have figured this out for myself.

It was too much; of all the rotten luck! Having listened to these two on the journey, I felt I would never know another minute's peace, and at this moment it was peace and silence for which I most fervently longed. All I wanted to do was to flop into bed and end the day.

I was aware of the constant prattle between Rosie and Mavis, despite the fact that I had plugged my ears with cotton wool. My bed was hard and uncomfortable; the mattress undulated like the Cheviot Hills, but with violent volcanic bumps more like the Grampians. The sheets were like cardboard, and the grey blankets unbending. Even my horse has a better blanket, I thought. The pillow, however, was the most intractable of all. If I slept a wink it would be a miracle was my last thought before I passed into oblivion.

*   *   *

"Bloody 'ell, wot the devil's that?" Rosie's voice was the first sound I heard.

"It's the rising bell," said Mavis. "I read on the Notice Board that it would ring at 6:45 a.m."

I just bet you did, I thought bitterly. Trust her to have spotted what no one else in their right mind or exhausted state would have seen. I had known this girl for only a few hours, and already I wanted to do her in.

I rolled slowly out of bed and pulled back the blackout curtains to see what lay outside. The elegant old city of Harrogate still dozed in the mists, and the hotel gardens were barely visible in the early light. What I could see was crisped with January frost.

I turned from the window and at that moment saw Rosie

pulling off her nightdress. At first I was not totally sure what it was she was encased in. Then, from my scanty memory of ladies' magazines, I realized it was a corset. There was a lot of Rosie to hold in, and it was sternly laced both front and back, giving the poor girl the devil's own job to pull up her stockings. She had obviously slept in it, which I would have thought to be pure torture. Standing there in that Victorian room, she looked exactly like a Toulouse Lautrec painting, with her vivid hair and more than opulent figure. I was suddenly aware that I must have been staring, and turned away quickly with a sense of guilt, as though I had intruded upon something painfully private.

Rosie, to my surprise, was totally unaware of anything bizarre, or that her corset was causing such interest. As she dressed, she chatted and chuckled, exclaimed and cursed in a kind of ceaseless flow, her only competition being the chirping of the frost-bitten little sparrows on the windowsill.

The door flew open, and in breezed a very smart, self-confident N.C.O.

"Good morning, everyone," she announced brightly. There were mumbled responses; as with the eyes at half mast, we stood limply about in stages of semi-undress.

She carried on in a hearty, games mistress sort of way. "Now I would like you all to watch very carefully while I show you how to make a bed in the correct W.A.A.F. fashion."

I was convinced it was all going to be a lot of military ado about nothing—any idiot could make a bed—until I began to discover the reason for my uncomfortable night. The Air Force did not call it "stacking a bed" for nothing. The whole operation had to be carried out with the utmost precision, and everything had to be in its correct place, including the mattress, which I now discovered was in three parts, known in the vernacular as "biscuits."

I stood mesmerized as I watched the corporal deftly arrange the bedding, ending up with an effect a bit like an

American club sandwich. I, of course, had attempted to sleep on my bed by pulling blankets and sheets out where I could find them, and thumping the mattress about to locate a comfortable valley. We were now warned solemnly that an untidy "stack" would not be tolerated. Improperly made, a bed would be pulled to pieces and the unlucky offender would be sent to do it again, possibly even put "on charge." I didn't have too much of a clue as to what being put on charge meant, but it sounded just a notch below hanging. Did the winning of the war depend upon a neat stack, I asked myself. Later on I realized it was all part of a necessary discipline, which was designed to give us pride of service, but on that first day it seemed, like everything else, totally irrelevant.

As we began struggling with this new art form, I heard the nutmeg-grater tones of Rosie: "Gor blimey, I've forgotten already how to stack this bloody bed."

I closed my eyes and waited for the inevitable. It was an invitation the dreaded Mavis could not pass up.

"It's easy," she said. "My sister joined a couple of months ago and taught me how to do it. Here, let me show you."

Finally, with much unsolicited help from Mavis, the beds were stacked and our room tidied. It was now time to find our way to the dining hall for breakfast.

I did not really notice what I was eating as, forever female, my mind was already dwelling pleasurably on the next step in the day's programme, which was the "kitting out."

I joined a rather straggling queue and eventually found myself face to face with a jolly, rotund R.A.F. flight sergeant. He had what could only be described as a practiced eye when it came to sizing up girls. He would rhyme off "36" or "40" after a brief appraisal of a recruit, and he was seldom wrong.

He looked me over with a cheery grin and handed me a pile of clothing. I took the kit over to the only free space in a room full of girls in various stages of undress and inspected my bundle. Somehow I had not expected the uniform to begin from the skin out. I divested myself of the few gossamer bits I was wearing and reached for the bra. It was made of thick, coarse cotton, with straps the width of a man's belt, and hooks and eyes so sturdy they could have been used to fasten the linen union covers of a three-piece suite. It was a hectic shade of pink, a sop, no doubt, to femininity.

The knickers were navy blue and knee length, and were apparently known colloquially as "blackouts" (as opposed, I later discovered, to our mufti ones which were dubbed "knockouts"). The stockings were thick grey lisle and had a decidedly convent air, as did the black regulation oxfords. The latter felt horribly clumsy when I first tried them on, but, as I walked about, turned out to be surprisingly comfortable.

When I finally got myself laced, hooked, buttoned, and belted, I turned to survey the result in the full-length mirror nearby. I looked and looked again. Was this tall, slim creature really me? It was not all that long ago that I had emerged from my coltish period, all arms and legs and wild masses of blonde hair. Now what I saw was a slenderly rounded version of the old me: the grey stockings stretched attractively; the Air Force blue did things for my colouring, and the hair had become a sleek roll under a dashing peaked cap. I was, not to put too fine a point on it, insufferably pleased with myself.

On the other side of the room, Rosie was waging war with a jacket several sizes too small.

"'Ere, Sergeant, I can't get me bloomin' buttons done up. Gor, I'm in a muck sweat! I'm tellin' you plain, so I am, if you can't find me a jacket wot fits, I'm effin' off and goin' 'ome."

What an extraordinary phrase I thought—"effin' off"—as stifled giggles spread through the room. I had never heard it before, and had no idea what it meant.

"No chance," replied the sergeant. "We can even find a jacket to fit Tessie O'Shea. Here, try this one."

When she did manage to get herself buttoned up, she contrived to look faintly armour-plated. The uniform was just not her style, and she appeared strangely at odds with herself, as though her personality had somehow been diminished. She was born to spend her life in feather boas and buttoned boots, I thought to myself.

Mavis did not fare much better, but at least she looked as though she belonged in her uniform, solidly belonged, I might say.

Once equipped, the next order of business was to polish up the brass buttons and buckles of our tunics. They had obviously never been within a mile of a tin of polish. If I had been feeling a bit smug about the svelte figure I cut, I was taken down a peg or two when it came to polishing buttons. The brass and copper at home may have gleamed, but certainly through no effort on my part. I was slopping away with the Brasso and flicking an ineffectual polishing rag about when I felt a nudge that nearly broke my ribs.

"Give it 'ere, girl," said Rosie, shaking her orange head in disgust. "I'll show you 'ow to do it."

She grabbed my jacket and proceeded to rub with such vigour that her whole ample being wobbled like jelly. She worked away for some time applying, quite literally, both spit and polish until, holding the jacket at arm's length, she nodded her satisfaction with the results and handed it back to me. No guardsman could have had a more glistening display than the row of buttons that now gleamed down my front like gold nuggets. I was overcome by her kindness, and felt ashamed at having pre-judged her by such snobbish standards.

"Thank you so much, Rosie, that was very kind of you," I began.

Rosie dismissed any further effusions with a wave of her plump hand and a shrug of her shoulders. "Blimey, they're sayin' somefink else," she said as another announcement came over the tannoy.

"Will all new recruits report to the desk to receive their numbers."

Once again, like a flock of sheep, led, of course, by the stocky figure of Mavis, the little tribe advanced towards the desk. A handsome R.A.F. sergeant, sporting a huge handlebar moustache, was waiting for us.

"All right, girls, form a queue. Before I call out yer numbers, I want to tell you that from now on, you 'aven't got a name no more, just yer number. You eat by number, get paid by number, go on leave by number, get put on charge by number, so if you don't know yer number, you don't flippin' well exist. Once you get yer number, go off and learn it—frontways, sideways, backways, any bloomin' way you wish, but *learn it!*"

Oh God, I thought, I'm hopeless with numbers. I can barely remember our telephone number. Numbers were being called out, and the long queue inched forward. Visions of myself wandering, numberless, in a kind of eternal no-man's-land panicked me, and by the time I reached the sergeant, I must have looked as though I were expecting a death sentence. He gave me a big smile and a reassuring wink.

"Yer number, me luv, is Aircraft Woman Second Class Number 427246."

He handed me a slip of paper with my rank and number, and I made a dash for the nearest toilet. I locked the door and leant against the white tiled wall, staring blankly at the piece of paper in my hand: 4-2-7 246, and again, 427 2-4-6. The last three digits were even numbers in sequence, but there was just no rhythm to the first three. I repeated them over again, very slowly and very deliberately, until I felt they were burnt into my mind. All the other important numbers in my life have long since fled, but I am convinced that I will be able to rhyme off *4 2 7 2 4 6* in my final hour.

The atmosphere amongst us was becoming more relaxed as the day wore on. We were beginning to find our own levels, and friendships were in the making. I met a pretty girl called Nancy, who was standing next to me in one of our many queues. She came from South America and had been to boarding school in Berkshire. Her father was Spanish, her mother English, and she seemed to have acquired the most attractive features of both. She was short, a little on the cuddly side, very vivacious, and had a lovely smile. We liked each other immediately. That evening was spent sewing name tapes onto all our new clothes. Being pretty deft with a needle, I was glad to be able to return the favour of the buttons and give Rosie a hand. These few tentative approaches were welcomed by both of us, and I knew a genuine bond of friendship was in the making. I could imagine my parents' reaction, particularly if I were to tell them what I was later to learn from Rosie.

We had been told that the following day we could all go into Harrogate to shop, and most important of all, buy postcards to send home announcing our safe arrival, and allaying any fears our parents might have about their fledglings. It was also vital to give them our new service numbers and correct rank, for as the sergeant said, "No numbers, no letters!"

Later on, we had to bundle up our civilian clothes to be sent on to our home addresses. It was the last act distancing ourselves from what we had been before.

Like prisoners hearing the gate shut and the key turn, we were locked into a system where we were numbers and did as we were told; our human likes, dislikes, fads, or even temperaments were not a matter for consideration. Furthermore, we were always together. Ever since childhood, I had loved to tuck myself away in my room for moments of necessary isolation. In that first day, I was to discover that solitude was an almost unattainable paradise, and those rare moments when it beckoned were to be cherished. One such opportunity, I found, was to make a dive for the bathroom, lock the door, and lie soaking and dreaming in the tub. It was positively luxurious, except for the thick, black plumb line painted on the bath, commanding that no one should draw water beyond this point.

It was a happy evening, hearing all the plans being laid for the following day's invasion of Harrogate. The Y.M.C.A. was mentioned several times, and the popular suggestion was that we should all meet up there in the evening, as our passes permitted us to be out until 9:45 p.m.

I was just putting my sewing kit away in my drawer when Rosie suddenly spoke up.

"Could I 'ave a word with you, girl?" she asked, leading me rather furtively into an empty corner of the room. "You was nice to me about them bloody tapes," she went on, "and I don't want you to take no offence, but I just couldn't live with myself if I didn't put you straight about one or two things."

I could not begin to think what horrible disclosures I was about to hear, and looked around hoping to rope a third person into this tête-à-tête. Unfortunately, everybody had left to go down to the Recreation Hall, and I was trapped here, alone with Rosie.

"First off, 'as yer mum 'ad a word with you?"

Memories of my mother's vague references to dates and drink floated to mind.

"I thought not," said Rosie after a look at my bemused expression. "Ye're just a kid, and I've got to admit I never 'ave seen a greener one. I might as well tell you, 'cos ye're likely to find out sooner or later, but I've been on the game!"

She paused for dramatic effect and I knew, out of politeness, I should say something, but what game could she be talking about? I seemed to remember Kipling referring to the Great Game in one of his books, and as I recalled, it dealt with high-level intelligence on the Northwest Frontier. It was inconceivable that Rosie could have been a spy.

"Er, what game was that, Rosie?" I asked hesitantly.

"Gor," she replied, her little eyes disappearing as she turned them in supplication toward heaven, "I knew it, I knew it . . . *the* game, I'm talking about. I was a tart, a prostitute, a bloody whore!"

I turned crimson and could not look at her.

"It's all right, ducks," she said not unkindly, "it's behind me now. I've made the break and it's a fresh start for Rosie, but I want you to understand that I know what I'm talkin' about. I know the ropes and I'm telling you, a pretty kid like you is ripe for pluckin' out of the tree, and so is that other little thing."

I guessed she was referring to Nancy.

"So," she went on, "whether you like it or not, I don't intend to let you out of my sight tomorrow when we go to 'Arrogate, especially at the Y.-bleedin'-M.C.A., or any other night come to that, until you can look after yerselves. These Y.M.C.A. dumps are pick-up joints and you have to be careful. So I'm sticking to you for yer own good, dearie, and that's that. No offence, mate?"

I was blushing to the roots of my hair, so completely was I taken aback. But I loved Rosie for her motherly concern, for she was right, and I knew it. In her eyes, I was totally inexperienced, in more ways than one, and I welcomed a stalwart like Rosie behind me. We left together to go and have a coffee and I felt just like Rosie's chick following in the wake of her ruffled and protective feathers.

Learning the Ropes

W E AWAKENED the next morning to a changed world. There had been a heavy fall of snow during the night, and the grey town had been transformed into a magical place of white velvet trees and diamond frost. The windows had been etched into delicate tapestries of forests and ferns and mountains, and, as usual, I went off into one of my Walter Mitty trances, dreaming of snow queens and ice-bound kingdoms.

The breakfast bell's piercing shriek brought me back to the reality of Harrogate and Room 504. "What a difference a day makes," I found myself singing. Far from yesterday's civilian chaos, our room was a model of military spiff: six neatly stacked beds and six immaculately dressed girls, shoes and buttons shined, stocking seams straight, and ready to pass the most exacting inspection.

Due to the snowy conditions, drill instruction had been cancelled, and in its place we were to be taught how to salute. Why, I asked myself, do we need a whole morning to learn to move one's hand outwardly from one's hat? Little did I guess that saluting was an art form to be honed and polished until it became a masterpiece of precision. The palm of the right hand must face forwards, straight fingers and thumb held tightly together so that no light could be seen between; the longest finger to be placed exactly one inch behind the side of the right eye on the temple.

We were divided into pairs to practice between ourselves, and there was many a muffled giggle as fingers poked eyes, and thumbs hooked into caps. It seemed an incredibly awkward manoeuvre that first day, yet within a week it would become as natural as breathing.

Saluting all morning made the afternoon's freedom all the more attractive. We were like puppies straining on the leash by the time we were ready to set out for town. Yet there was one more trick to learn before we could leave. We had to be passed as being properly attired: great coats buttoned up to the neck, caps on at regulation position, dead straight and tilted slightly forward. We were also given the first of many "little talks" about the honour, behaviour and general decorum required of a W.A.A.F. So much for any ideas we may have had of larking in the snow.

We had divided into two groups, the girls of Room 504 falling naturally together. Rosie, faithful to her promise, sallied forth like a galleon under full sail, with Nancy and me in her wake. The slippery snow made walking difficult, and as we approached a steep hill, I noticed three R.A.F. officers approaching.

"Quick," I said, "we've got to salute these officers. Crumbs, what do we do? It *is* the right hand, isn't it?"

"Yes, yes," hurried the others, "are you ready?"

With that, three smart W.A.A.F.'s raised their right arms and gave three cracking salutes. It was a matchless performance, and we were inwardly congratulating ourselves when we were aware that Rosie was in motion. In the enthusiasm of her salute, she had lost her balance, slipped in the snow, and flew in an almost perfect parabolic curve to land with the most horrendous bump on her backside, her cap careering wildly down the road.

It should have been filmed in slow motion, but actually it all happened in less than a second. The three officers (and gentlemen) went to her assistance most charmingly, but it was all too much for Rosie—she cursed and swore like a fishwife as she dusted herself off. All the while the R.A.F. officers, without displaying the slightest flicker of amusement, brushed her down and collected her cap before continuing on their way. This could not be said for us W.A.A.F.'s, whose suppressed laughter showed in our faces. It was like a Laurel and Hardy comedy, and we managed to walk with decorum until rounding the bend, when we gave way to uncontrollable laughter.

Nonetheless, I was braced and ready for a "Lesson in Life" as we approached Rosie's den of iniquity, the Y.M.C.A., later on that evening. As we came through the door, we were greeted by wolf whistles and provocative comments.

"You both keep with me, " muttered Rosie darkly as we made our way to the counter. "Now then, what will you 'ave?"

"Let's have coffee and doughnuts all 'round," I said, though heaven knows why, as I had always loathed doughnuts. Somewhere in the back of my mind I must have cherished the notion that it was what one was supposed to order in canteens.

We made our way across the room to a free table, and before we even had the chance to sit down, three soldiers appeared from nowhere, bowing in exaggerated politeness and holding our chairs.

"Hello, girls," they grinned, "do you mind if we join you?"

"Bloody right we do," snapped back Rosie.

"Don't be like that, gorgeous, we only want to be friendly."

"Now you just shut yer cakehole and go be friendly somewhere else," she retorted, dismissing them with a turn of her back.

"Okay, okay. I guess we know when we're not wanted."

Despite Rosie's far from gracious treatment, the trio was obviously not crushed. In a matter of a few minutes they were chatting up some A.T.S. girls with a lot more success.

"There now, do you girls see wot I mean? Just because ye're wearing a skirt, that's all— don't matter wot yer face looks like— they just home in on you like bloody pigeons. Just give 'em the push, you hear. You be the one to do the choosin', otherwise with all these blokes around, yer life won't be worth callin' yer own. They've only got one bloody thing on their minds, mark my words. If a bloke is nice enough, 'e won't offer all 'e's got on a plate in the first ruddy sentence. But there," she wound up, "you'll soon learn to sort them out. Just remember to watch out for the artful dodgers."

I managed a wink at Nancy without Rosie seeing me. She had taken on her broody hen look, and worked herself up into quite a state, carried away no doubt by her own eloquence. Her cheeks were flushed, and her vivid hair was falling down in indignant strands on her collar, but at that moment I felt such a rush of affection I could have hugged her.

* * *

The general training programme began the next day, and over the weeks that followed we grew slowly from a heterogeneous collection of civilians into a smart, well-disciplined squad.

Throughout this time we were being assessed as to our skills and attitudes with a view to eventual job selection. For most of us it was also a period of self-assessment, discovering as we did unsuspected strengths and weaknesses, as well as surprising degrees of adaptability. We found ourselves accepting orders and rules, at first in a spirit of resignation, then with growing enthusiasm, and finally with a determination to match ourselves individually and collectively to the challenge.

At the end of the first three weeks, our group was split up and sent to two other units on the outskirts of Harrogate. Both had been boys' boarding schools and were known as Ash Vale and Pannal Ash. Rosie and I were posted to Pannal Ash, and sadly Nancy was sent to Ash Vale. I hated to see her go, as I had rather unreasonably envisioned us marching side by side throughout the entire war. It was my first experience in handling the disruption of friendship that service life can bring.

Once settled into the austere and dubious comfort of Pannal Ash, we were assigned our duties. "Duties" was really an up-market word for what were the lowest and most menial of tasks. I began to feel a little like a Dickensian urchin, bound for life to a mountain of potatoes and an ocean of unwashed floors. Strangely enough, while most of the girls railed against this regime, I found myself rather enjoying it. It was all so completely novel to me, and part of what I dramatically thought of as "Experience."

My enthusiasm cooled a little when I was detailed to clean the toilets— eighty in all. The Air Force did not go in for the delicate little dusting of Harpic the loos received at home. I was instructed that I must shove my entire arm in, up, and over the U-bend. Nobody told me the why of all this probing; I was just assured by a fearsome senior N.C.O. that at all costs I must go round the bend.

For ten days, I spent the better part of each morning practically standing on my head, my arm disappearing over the U-bend. The surrounding porcelain also had to gleam like a new moon, and the old wooden seats be made to shine. I then had to scrub the floor and wash down the doors. All this effort was later meticulously examined, not by the overseeing N.C.O. but by a W.A.A.F. officer. At this point in my burgeoning career, I made a mental note that if I ever got to be an officer, it was not to be as an inspector of toilets. There had to be better things to do with a commission.

On one occasion, I found one of the toilets blocked to overflowing. I reported this at once to my N.C.O., who in turn fetched an R.A.F. plumber. He rooted around for some time, then fished something out and held it up for my inspection.

"That's your problem, Miss. Get the N.C.O. to put up a notice telling the girls not to put their sanitary towels down the lavatories."

I longed to die on the spot. I was crimson with embarrassment at being confronted by a man— a man, of all things— holding up this most intimate of female necessities. He, on the other hand, did not turn a hair. It was all part of the job, and he was as blasé as a doctor asking questions of a naked lady.

The second chapter in "My Life Downstairs" was spent beside Rosie, peeling sackfuls of potatoes. Rosie grumbled incessantly as she viciously attacked one spud after another. Whereas I, inexperienced in potato peeling, set about my task with a liberal hand and treated the whole thing as an enormous joke. Or at least I did until the sergeant came over to inspect our work. He took one look at my bucketful and swung around, fixing me eyeball to eyeball with a ferocious glare.

"Good God, girl," he shouted, "have you never peeled potatoes before? Bloody useless you look to me. You're cutting them the thickness of my shoe sole. If you go on like this, we'll lose the bleeding war on your wastage alone. You'll have to do better than this, I can tell you. All right then, you'll stay on for another hour on your own. Do you hear me?" he bellowed as I hung my head in silence.

"Yes, Sergeant," I replied meekly, feeling utterly crushed.

As he walked away, Rosie gave me a kindly nudge. "Never mind, ducks. 'Is bark is worse than 'is bite. I'll make yer bed, then we'll nip out to the pub for a quick one, as soon as ye're finished."

With Rosie gone, I had time to think about my disgrace. It was true, I had been larking about, and it would be bound to show up on my final assessment. If I had to begin by mastering the art of peeling potatoes, then master it I would. The first necessity was obviously a really sharp knife. Also, I thought, it would not do any harm to show the sergeant that I was both contrite and ready to learn. I approached him a bit hesitantly and asked him if he would be kind enough to sharpen my knife. He seemed surprised but was only too pleased to oblige.

At the end of the hour, I was amazed to see the pile of potatoes I had waded through. The peelings were tissue thin, and I looked at them with almost affectionate pride. I left the kitchens with an approving nod from the sergeant, and as soon as I was out of view, dashed to join Rosie on our trip to the pub.

I had only been in one pub so far in my life, and that had been with Donald after watching him play in a cricket match. Both teams had piled into a quaint little inn on the village green. It was a humpty-dumpty sort of structure, with a thick, thatched roof and a cozy, beamed interior, very much like something out of a *Beautiful Britain* calendar.

Nothing could have been further from that charming local than the pub Rosie and I now entered. It was a red brick monster, noisy and brash, and thick with smoke. As we elbowed our way towards the bar, I felt ill at ease and alien as a Martian. Rosie, on the other hand, was opening up like a sunflower after the rain. As I knew, there were places where she was at odds with her environment, but not here. I remember following her through the crowd and marvelling at her natural friendliness, her sharp cockney wit, and her magical way with people. Within minutes we were surrounded.

"Look 'ere," she proclaimed delightedly, "you blokes don't push in so damned close. We're not bloody monkeys in a zoo. Move back and give us some air for Gawd's sake."

Through it all, she kept an eye on me, watching for a straying hand or a too suggestive suggestion. At the end of the evening I returned to the barracks aware that I had been watching a master at work, and that my training in the art of controlling advances was coming on apace.

The following week was to see the last of our skivvy chores. After this, we would be allocated to a particular branch of the service, and intensive, specialized training would begin.

In these concluding weeks, however, I found my final task was to clean the billet. This consisted of three vast, sprawling floors, linked by a never-ending spiral staircase. The wretched stairs were not carpeted, of course, but covered in linoleum. It was my job to polish them—and the adjoining hallways—until the whole shone like crystal. Rosie, who had been assigned this task earlier, confided in me that the W.A.A.F. officer in charge was a gold-plated bitch and a demon over details.

She had not exaggerated. At the end of my first day, I was up on the carpet and subjected to a scathing review of my efforts.

"It just will not do, young woman. You will have to perform much better than this, or you will be kept in on fatigue duty tomorrow. And," she concluded offensively, "for heaven's sake put some elbow grease into it."

No matter how poor the results, I had worked like a Trojan on those terrible stairs, and I seethed with fury. I looked at her retreating back with loathing. I raged inwardly. If she wants a polish, I'll give her a polish that will send her sailing from top to bottom.

Little did I realize that my thoughts would be translated so prophetically. The next morning as I finished polishing the bottom step, I heard the sound of voices and footsteps approaching along the upper corridor. The officer and her N.C.O.'s were on their daily inspection. As they rounded the bend to make their way down the stairs, there was a sudden shriek, followed by bumps and crashes, and then an ominous silence. I slunk into the broom cupboard and peered through a slit in the door. N.C.O.'s were flying down the stairs. The officer picked herself up, reset her cap, adjusted her tunic and set off—albeit with something less than her usual assurance—down the stairs. I regret to say it, but it was probably one of the sweetest moments of my life. Vengeance may belong to the Lord, but He managed to share a little of it with me that day.

Special Duties

OUR DAYS in Harrogate were almost over. We were about to be split up again and sent off to different training camps. Once more, we had to face the sadness of leaving people and places that had become important to us.

On the final day, we all crowded into the assembly hall where the allocations were to be announced. Mine was finally called out. "Aircraftwoman Second Class 427246—Special Duties."

I had not the slightest idea what it meant, but felt it carried an ongoing sense of mystery, as though I had just unwrapped the first layer of tissue from an intriguing parcel. So many of these assignments were self-explanatory, like "cook" or "clerk" or "M.T. driver," but "Special Duties" had a mystique, faintly secret and very important. Twenty-eight others were also in this category, and we were told that we would only get to know about the job itself when we arrived at our training destination.

Rosie was not among the twenty-eight, and I found saying good-bye to her worse than I had imagined. She had become my friend in the truest sense of the word, and yet I knew somehow, despite our mutual promises to keep in touch, that we would never see each other again.

The lorry arrived in time to save me from tears, and we all piled in. We could only guess at our destination, but knew that we were travelling south—London, perhaps, headquarters, top brass? This pleasurable speculation ended when the lorry stopped and our point of arrival was announced: Leighton Buzzard, Bedfordshire! Leighton Buzzard? Glamour slipped from my thoughts like a cloak crumpling to the floor.

We arrived in total darkness and rather disconsolately got out of the lorry. Looming through the dark was a very large and gaunt Victorian building complex. It was, in fact, an old workhouse, and the only thing missing was Oliver Twist with his bowl of gruel. The thick snow did nothing to soften the grim outlines of this forbidding structure, and I felt as though it were daring us to enter.

However, we had little choice in the matter and went through into one of the two blocks that faced each other on either side of a large quadrangle. We were led into a temporary guard room and there were greeted by a W.A.A.F. flight sergeant who looked as though she should have been baking scones in some country kitchen. She was round and cuddly, and seemed to radiate kindness and goodwill. I could not help wondering whether some Air Force casting director had selected her especially to offset the bleakness of the surroundings.

She led us away to be further comforted by a good meal and a hot drink. It was not long before things began to relax, and conversation to flow. Although all of us had been at Harrogate, the numbers there had been such that most of us had never met, and it was just like the first day all over again.

Once dinner was over, the flight sergeant explained that whilst we would all be living at the workhouse, we would not be doing our training here. Instead, we would march two miles every day to a secret establishment for intensive training and return here in the evenings. She added that "intensive" was the operative word, and as a result we would have to be in our billets by 8:30 every night except Fridays and Saturdays, when we would be permitted late passes until 11 p.m.

When we had been briefed, we were escorted into the dormitory blocks. The upper floors were accessible only by an iron staircase on the outside of the buildings. Each block had an exterior gallery, and along this were rows of doors opening into individual rooms. There were no toilets or washing facilities, the ablutions block being a separate building in the centre of the quadrangle. Thank God, I thought, for a good bladder. The prospect of stumbling down those slippery, snow-covered iron stairs and across the icy quadrangle in the dead of night was too awful to contemplate.

The rooms themselves were small and bare, but with one major item of comfort. This was a small, upright coke fire, whose stack went up through the roof and presumably into a chimney. The heat it was generating, as the six of us trooped into our assigned room, was like a benediction. This funny little heater created a sort of coziness despite the stark surroundings, as we gathered around it on that first night, holding out our hands like the lost boys in Peter Pan, and sharing its companionable warmth.

We had been told we would be spending four weeks here, and I could hardly wait to tell my parents that I was living in a workhouse, if for no other reason than to vie with my father and his cell at Wormwood Scrubs. He, at least, does not have to brave icy winds and drifts of snow to get to the loo, I thought bitterly the next morning, as I set out at 6:30 for the facilities. I was reminded of the rigours of boarding school as I dabbed my way through a cold bath before returning to stack my bed and help clean the billet.

After breakfast, we all fell in on the quadrangle and were formed into squads for our march into the unknown. We moved briskly through the little town of Leighton Buzzard and on out into the countryside. Some two miles later, we were given the command of "right turn" and entered through a set of impressive gates guarded by R.A.F. personnel.

Suddenly I was aware that the sky had disappeared: the frosty blue of the winter heavens had been replaced by mile after mile of green camouflage netting. There was no question about it, this was true top secret stuff, and I was relishing the thought.

The long shrouded driveway led up to what appeared to

be a substantial country house. We were ushered into a large room, in the centre of which was a massive table covered with a green baize cloth. An R.A.F. officer was waiting for us. He invited us to sit down and then proceeded to tell us why we were there.

"You girls," he began, "are about to be trained as plotters to work with Fighter Command, probably at their headquarters at Bentley Priory in Middlesex. Now the word 'plotter' will have no meaning for you at this stage, so it is going to be my job to enlighten you. Before we begin your training, however, you will be required to take an oath of secrecy. I cannot stress too strongly the secretive nature of this work. You will be asked to swear on oath that you will never mention what you are doing to another human being—parent, husband, brother, sister, boyfriend, the man in the street, or the barmaid in the pub. Should you ever break this oath, either deliberately or through indiscretion, you will be dishonourably discharged. Have I made myself clear?"

How could he possibly ask if he had made himself clear? Chinese torture would not have induced me to say what I had eaten for breakfast, let alone divulge the nation's secrets. I was thrilled beyond measure. Was it possible that only a few weeks ago, the chief things on my mind had been riding, and dressing up to look pretty for a date? Now here I was, part of some vast secret plan to destroy the enemy and win the war.

As soon as our training began, I realized why it had to be kept so secret. It was absolutely fascinating, and I was devastated when I developed a severe chill within a day or two of our arrival. My chest seemed cased in iron, my head and throat ached, and I felt like death. It was agony to make that two-mile march in sub-zero temperatures every day, but I was petrified that if I had said how awful I felt, I might be forced out of training and subsequently dropped from the course. It was unthinkable, and I begged my friends to say nothing. They were marvellous and rallied around with endless hot drinks and inhalations. I spent the weekend under a towel inhaling menthol crystals, and doctored myself with massive applications of the Air Force cure-alls, Gees Linctus and Mist Expect. Whether it was the treatment or a lot of prayer to the Almighty, I emerged on Monday shaky but recovered.

During the rest of our training, I found the work so absorbing that I had little time for anything else. Being a swat has its compensations, however, for much to my delight I passed the first half of the course with the highest marks.

The Beehive

I T WAS time to move on again. Only twelve of us were being sent to Fighter Command headquarters, and once more reluctant farewells were said, once more we clambered into an R.A.F. lorry with our treasures packed tightly into our kit bags. This transfer was a major one, because we now were going, not as raw recruits, but as fully fledged Aircraft Women Second Class.

We found on our arrival at Bentley Priory that it was a vast camp, with an enormous population, really more like a small town than an R.A.F. station. I think we all felt a bit intimidated and more than a little insignificant when we jumped down from the lorry that first day.

Our billets were known as "huts," and that is exactly what they were—long, low wooden structures, wherein we ate and slept. They were to be our home for nearly two years. Despite war, deprivation, and tragedy, they were, in retrospect, possibly the two happiest years of my life. Maybe fulfillment is a better word than happiness. I only know that the war, and the challenge of the work I was doing, intensified every reaction and emotion, and that I was living life on the mountaintop.

We were divided into watches, alternating day with night watches, each one a week's duration: 1 a.m. to 5 a.m. or 5 a.m. to 9 a.m. Day watches were: 9 a.m. to 1 p.m.; 1 p.m. to 5 p.m., and 5 p.m. to 9 p.m. With these shifts, life in the huts was a constant coming and going, girls on one shift hardly ever coming into contact with their counterparts.

We had to take a ten-minute coach ride to get to the

Operations room, and I can still remember the sense of awe I had when I saw it for the first time. It was forty-five feet below ground, and honeycombed with corridors. Apart from the Operations Room, there were offices, vast telephone exchanges, canteens and rest rooms, and through them all, people moved like an enormous and rhythmic army of bees.

Fresh from training, I was itching to get started as we were shown into the Filter Operations room. The layout was identical to the room in which we had done our training at Leighton Buzzard. The difference was that this was the real thing, and mistakes could not, and would not, be tolerated.

I glanced around the room and was immediately struck by the remarkable number of very pretty girls positioned around the table. I learned later that quite a number of them had been recruited from the Cochran girls of London stage fame, the equivalent of the Bluebell girls of today, and I began to wonder if plotters had been carefully hand-picked purely for reasons of decor.

Looks aside, we soon found a very high degree of competence was required. After the first agonizing nervousness disappeared, confidence grew, and as we gained experience and speed, we were promoted to map locations around the table where the heavier air battles were taking place. The greatest accolade was to be positioned on Dover, where the intensity of the dogfights was relentless. Sometimes a girl on this position could not be relieved of her watch until the air battles died down, so concentrated and constant was the activity. It took me five months to be positioned on Dover, and my pride on that day was unbounded.

We were not, however, without our moments of light relief. One of the stations which gave plot positions to Fighter Command was a naval post at Fareham. The officers there were on a specialized course, and indulged in a little relaxation by chatting up the girls at the other end of the line. The first time I was plugged into Fareham, I drew a regular spellbinder. His name was Kenneth Dibden, he said, from Harpenden near St. Albans, where his father-was a vicar. Whether his parents would have approved or not, son Kenneth was blessed with a golden tongue and was soon sweet-talking me into a date.

"Will you meet me in London tomorrow?" he asked. "I'll bring a friend and you bring one, too. We can meet under the clock at Waterloo Station at twelve noon."

I had never had a blind date before, but I felt I should be on pretty safe ground if I took a friend with me. My heart was pounding as I heard myself reply, "All right, we'll be there. I'll look forward to seeing you tomorrow."

What had I done, and what would my parents say if they knew? I had little time to dwell on the matter, as a dogfight had started overhead, and for the rest of my watch, I concentrated on the hell that was going on in the skies.

I had become very friendly with a marvellous girl called Liz, and on the coach going back to our billets I broached the matter of a double blind date. She jumped at the idea, and we spent an exciting evening wondering what the men would be like. Certainly Kenneth's voice was divine, I assured her, adding that I only hoped it matched his looks.

The next day we set off for London in a fever of anticipation and duly arrived at Waterloo, positioning ourselves at 12 noon under the big clock. In a last-minute attack of nerves, Liz wondered if it might be wiser to stand a little way off and give them the once-over, in case they were absolute freaks. Too late, here they were walking towards us, two dashing naval lieutenant commanders. They both were everything any pair of starry-eyed young females could have dreamed of— handsome, gallant, and great fun.

As could be imagined, it was a wonderful evening, and the first of many. It was also the first of many similar future entanglements. It seemed so easy in those days to slip into relationships which too rapidly assumed an intensity to match the times. Kenneth was a charmer— even my mother was entranced— but the last thing I wanted was any form of commitment. My new life was too exciting and challenging to give up, and so as Kenneth became more and more serious, I found myself retreating. Inevitably, our relationship ended, with pain on his part and a sense of loss on mine.

With Kenneth in mind, I tried hard to keep my dates light and friendly. Yet as the weeks slipped into months, I found it increasingly difficult to maintain an even balance in my social life. For one thing, the ratio of male to female was very much in our favour, and most of us were deluged with offers of dates. I loved going out and being flattered and treated like the only girl in the world, but I shied away from involvement.

On one occasion when plotting, I glanced up to see a group of fighter pilots standing up in the balcony, staring down at the grid map. A minute or so later, I was aware of a piece of paper fluttering down beside my chair. When there was a lull in the plotting, I picked it up and read: "I never could resist blue eyes. Will you have dinner with me tonight? My name is Ben. Please ring me at London 06249 at 5 p.m."

I was not sure that I should glance up again, but being a woman, nothing short of a Nazi invasion would have stopped me. I looked up to see an incredibly handsome flying officer grinning down at me. After approximately two seconds of soul searching, I decided to take him up on his invitation, but not alone. Liz and I had made a pact never to accept a date offer unless we went together. I later managed to locate her and the two of us walked over to the telephone box to make the call.

"Hello, it's me, Muriel. You showered me with paper this morning, do you remember?"

He assured me that he remembered me only too vividly, and a foursome was duly arranged. Once again feelings of guilt and parental disapproval assailed me. I countered these with the sensible thought that there could be no possible harm in a simple little dinner invitation.

They arrived at our billets in a snappy little M.G. It would have provided a tight squeeze for two, and proved extremely matey for four. Nobody could maintain a remote dignity while packed into a two-seater sports car, and the ice was broken within the first few minutes. In the course of the evening, we discovered that they were stationed at Biggin Hill, and were on a forty-eight-hour leave. That they intended to make the fullest possible use of the leave, however, did not come home to us until our return to the billets.

We arrived just before midnight—the time stamped on our passes—and it was then I heard the first faint tinkling of a warning bell. As we left the car and were making our way slowly in the darkness toward the gate, I realized that my handsome escort was taking things a bit *too* much for granted. Suddenly the image of Rosie was there between us, and with an almighty push, I managed to disengage myself. He was utterly flabbergasted as I went on to tell him furiously that I had no intention of carrying on like that and was sorry if I had given him that impression, but there it was.

Through all this diatribe, I was horribly aware of sounding like a prissy schoolgirl. I fully anticipated his asking me what I expected, having accepted an invitation from a stranger. Surprisingly enough, he did not but instead apologized, saying he had behaved like a mongrel, and would I ever forgive him, and how much he wanted to see me again. He went on at such a preposterous length that we both burst out laughing and ended up with a kiss at the door.

I saw Ben fairly often after that, until he was shot down and captured a few months later. It was painful to think of that free spirit in captivity, and I often pictured him going over the wire in a flurry of bullets and a baying of hounds.

D for Donald

THE DAY that the leave list was pinned on the notice board, the entire billet erupted. Everyone was pushing and shoving, each hoping to see her name posted. Liz made it through the melee, and shouted back that we were both on. Three whole precious days, starting as of that moment. We had been on night watch and had just come off at 5 a.m. There obviously was not a second to lose.

"If we hurry," Liz called over her shoulder while throwing a few necessities into a hold-all, "we can catch the first tube train from Stanmore at 6:30."

Breakfast was a useless exercise, as we were both too high on excitement to eat. We set off down the road in the light of the fading moon and arrived at Stanmore, after a good half hour's walk, just as dawn was breaking. It was still very early when we reached Waterloo, and I saw for the first time how the people of London were waging war. Almost every inch of platform space was covered with domestic paraphernalia: thermoses and primus stoves, baby carry-cots, sheets, and blankets. They were waking up now, gathering their tattered reserves of strength for another day at the docks or in munitions factories or wherever. They must have been exhausted, but to see them they could have been on a day's excursion to Margate. They sang as they set up canteens, boiled kettles, and fed babies. I found my eyes pricking with tears at their unpretentious gallantry and courage.

I said good-bye to Liz and caught the train for Guildford. I had a penchant for surprises and had decided against telephoning the family with news of my weekend pass. As I walked up the steep incline of Warren Road, the anticipation of my first homecoming in my new uniform was almost uncontainable. It was still early in the morning, with the promise of a lovely spring day ahead. The road was almost empty, and so still I could hear every note of the birds in the hedgerows. I felt like "Pippa Passes"—"the year's at the spring, and the day's at the morn"—my heart singing with the joy of coming home.

At last I came to the entrance gate of Warren Farm House and turned into the familiar drive, the paddocks stretching out on either side. The grass still held the dew, and it shone like tears in the morning sunlight. Looking toward the house, I saw old Pluto slowly walking up the drive, as yet unaware that I was at the other end.

"Pluto," I called, "come here, boy." His ears pricked up, he looked in my direction, and with an ecstatic yelp came barreling up the driveway as I came running down it. We collided in a frantic exchange of hugs, pats, and licks. Pluto was one of my oldest and best friends, and he had given me a king's welcome. I felt tears on my cheeks.

I looked up, my hand still on Pluto's head, to see my mare, Sally, at the far end of the paddock, munching contentedly on the lush grass. I called out to her: "Sal, over here, girl."

She recognized the voice that she had not heard for weeks, but did not quite trust herself to believe it.

"Sal," I called again. "It's me, Muriel."

Slowly Sally raised her head, her ears went up, and with a soft neigh she trotted at speed towards the fence where her most devoted human friend stood waiting. I put my arms around her neck and clasped her head to mine. The lump returned to my throat, and I began to wonder if I were going to cry through this entire leave.

The silence was broken by Diana, my younger sister, who was walking up the drive with a bucket of food for Sally. With a whoop, she put down the bucket and ran into my outstretched arms. Diana had always been very special to me, rather like a real live baby doll. I had been thirteen when she was born, and always had the feeling that she had been created for me to play with. I swung her round and round, then the two of us hurried toward the house. The doors were never locked, and we burst into the kitchen to find my mother and Nellie arranging the day's menus. Our reunion was one of those moments of pure and undiluted happiness that come so rarely and stay with us forever.

Diana saddled up Sally and Stjarni, and like old times we set off together with all the dogs in tow to visit my favourite haunts, taking a picnic lunch with us. We wandered down remembered lanes and galloped across the downs. The freedom was beyond description, and the war was a world away. Yet I could not entirely escape. I was a different person from the girl who had left all those months ago. Looking up at the fighter planes on their way to Dover, I found myself being pulled back to the map grid, plotting the duels in the sky. For a moment the thought clouded my day, but it was impossible to think of death and destruction on this flawless April morning, with Diana prattling away at my side.

That evening the telephone rang, and I could hear my mother saying that yes, I was at home for three days. Who on earth could that be, I wondered. My mother came into the room, smiling: "It's for you, darling," she said.

I lifted the receiver. "Hello," I said rather tentatively.

"Moo, it's me, Donald, remember? I thought if you were going to be in, I would pop over and see how my best girl looks in her uniform."

Suddenly, I was all pulse. It was Donald . . . my Donald . . . Donald home, when I thought him a thousand miles away. What a day, I exulted, oh thank you God for this day. Donald was still talking. "Well, is it all right? May I come over?"

"Of course, of course, come right away, come now," I babbled. "I'll meet you at the top of the drive."

I changed back into my uniform, flicked a comb through

my hair, and ran up the drive with my feet barely touching the ground. I perched myself on the topmost rung of the five-bar gate, legs dangling and my heart pounding. I heard his little M.G. before it turned the corner into view, and as he drew nearer, I was only aware of his blue eyes searching me out. He looked more handsome than ever in his Fleet Air uniform. If he had worn it to dazzle, he had certainly succeeded.

I did not jump down from the gate but sat there balanced somewhat precariously, and feeling just a little bit shy. It had been five months since we last met, and the continuity of our old relationship had been disturbed. I smiled at him. "Hello, Don," I said, "welcome home."

He looked up at me and grinned, holding his arms out. Without thought, I was in them and kissing him as though I were afraid he would disappear.

"Moo, darling," he said after we had finally broken apart, "you can't even begin to imagine how much I've missed you. Enough to know that I want to ask you to marry me when this blasted war is over. Will you wait for me?"

I was moved to tears. I leaned forward and pulled his head down to mine. "Oh, Don, of course I will wait for you—forever if necessary. I only hope I can be loyal to you and you to me."

He let out a sigh of relief. "I'm not asking you to get up on a pedestal, Moo. We are both too young for that, and you must have some fun. I just want us to have something to hold onto and believe in, that's all."

We arranged to meet that same evening. Donald had to return to his ship the next day, but for tonight there was to be no war, and no pain of separation. Before coming over, he had reserved a table for the dinner dance at the Oatlands Park Hotel, and I sang as I got dressed and sprayed myself with scent.

It was an enchanted evening, the stuff young dreams are made of before life's realities rob us of both youth and dreams. We danced and danced. We danced until the chairs were piled onto the tables and the orchestra packed away their instruments. Finally, we too reluctantly left and drove slowly home. Before we said good-bye, Donald pulled out a little box and asked me to open it. My fingers were trembling a little as I pulled out a fine gold chain, from which hung a golden initial *D*. He fastened it around my neck, the initial lying against my heart.

"It's the way I want to remember you," he said, and I thought my heart would break. We were so young, and it was all so sad. For a moment, I tasted bitterness, thinking this is not the way life is supposed to be. We should have a golden summer of engagement ahead, and excited parents and a dreamy wedding.

Donald left in the morning and my three days' leave melted away. I was desperately disappointed not to have seen my father, who had recently been posted to Woodstock, near Oxford, and could not get home. However, sad as I was to leave my family, I was excited at the prospect of returning to my fascinating work. Besides, now that my probation period was finished and I was being upgraded to AirCraftwoman First Class, I knew I would be entitled to regular and more frequent leaves.

Christmas Present

LIZ AND I had arranged to meet so we could return to the base together, and there she was waiting for me under the same clock at Waterloo where we had met our naval officers. We both had so much to tell one another, and were still talking when we arrived back at the base. We had just enough time to have supper and then catch the coach that would take us on watch.

In the months that followed, I became increasingly thankful that I had a friend like Liz. Not only did we have a great deal in common, but for both of us it was a release valve to have a sympathetic listener in whom we could confide. We agreed that we would try to stick together and planned our moves accordingly, hoping for the best within the exigencies of wartime service. We managed to attain our corporal's stripes together, and were overjoyed when we discovered that we were both to be sent on a Corporal's Course to St. Athans, near Barry in Wales.

We set off for Wales in high spirits, but we had not bargained on being held up in London, along the route, by heavy bombing. The journey, in fact, turned into a nightmare, with prolonged stops, changing trains twice to make detours, no food or hot drinks, and arctic conditions on the train itself. All these annoyances dampened our enthusiasm more than a little, and we arrived at St. Athans in the pre-dawn hours, exhausted, very cold, and ravenously hungry.

We were warmed, physically and emotionally, by an effusive welcome, but even more so by the suggestion that we spend the rest of the night in sick bay, and sleep in the next morning. What an enormously civilized attitude, I thought, as I sank gratefully into bed.

The girls we met the next morning seemed equally friendly, and St. Athans was beginning to look better and better. This was just as well, as we would be there for a whole month, with Christmas thrown in for good measure.

The month turned out to be one of the hardest and most demanding I was to know in the Air Force. However, I had always loved challenges, and furthermore I truly enjoyed drill, dreaming of commanding a squad of my own some day. To my delight, drilling was a major part of our day's activities, the evenings being spent in writing up notes and studying. There was precious little time for recreation, except for a general relaxation of the rules over the four-day Christmas holiday. It was the first time I had not been with my family during the festive season, but it was impossible to feel lonely. We were part of a closely-knit and enormous clan, most of whom were bent on making Christmas Present as merry as any Christmas Past or Future, for that matter. There were dances every night in a choice of canteens, and what was even better, with a choice of partners, the men outnumbering the girls three to one.

Not long after Christmas, the course results were posted up on the notice board, and I could not believe it when I saw I had come through with a Highly Recommended and an average of 94 percent. Liz had done well, too, and we hugged each other in elation, congratulated ourselves backwards and forwards, and gloated over how proud everyone would be when we returned to Fighter Command.

We were sent off laden with good wishes, and as warmly as we had been welcomed. We had hoped for a smooth return trip to London, but it was as though the Germans had heard we were coming and had decided to give us another nightmare journey. There were bombings and disruptions, and changing of trains. Finally we were squeezed into a carriage occupied by members of the Irish Guards.

The cigarette smoke was dense, the laughter loud, and the jokes raucous. Our invasion was greeted with cheers and exaggerated courtesies, and suddenly the whole trip began to take on a different complexion. There was a lot of banter and merriment on both sides, in the midst of which someone started to tease us about the peaks of our caps, saying how awful they looked, and if he only had a needle and thread, he could alter them to look just like Guardsmen's caps. Liz promptly challenged him by sweeping off her cap and handing it over. Needles and thread were produced from somewhere, and before we knew it, the peak had been whipped from the cap, then pushed back in, leaving only a small amount showing. Stitching it in was another matter, as needle after needle broke on the strong backing. The finished product, however, was worth every curse and every pricked finger. A rather dowdy cap had been transformed into a truly dashing bit of headgear. By now everyone was mad keen to create the same effect, and the rest of the journey was spent passing needles around and bashing in peaks. We arrived back at the base in caps of unparalleled chic and totally non-regulation.

A few weeks later I was chosen for the cover of a *London Illustrated* issue boosting recruitment for the W.A.A.F. I was just heading off for the photographer's when the Station Warrant Officer stopped me, exclaiming, "Corporal, what on earth have you done to your cap? It looks absolutely frightful. Have you been bending it—the peak is almost touching your nose. Do try and do something about it, please, before you are photographed."

How could I tell her that I either went before the nation as I was, or in a cap punctuated with the most enormous needle holes!

1942

The Royal Bath

WHILE I was still on the Corporal's Course at St. Athans, the blitz on London was at its height. The Germans had stepped up the nightly bombings on an appalling scale, and the stories that reached us were terrifying. I was beginning to worry about my family, not all that far south of London. Letters were taking so long to arrive, and I could only pray that everything was all right. I decided to telephone home, as I felt that I must make some contact with my family, particularly my mother, coping alone as she was with everything at Warren Farm House. I wanted her to know I was thinking about her, and I also wanted to pass on the good news that at the end of my course I would be given two weeks' leave.

I had given this leave a lot of thought, and decided that for one of the weeks, I should swank it up at the Royal Bath Hotel in Bournemouth. I saw myself sweeping through its elegant doors, a woman of the world—self-assured, sophisticated, and just a trifle mysterious. It was a nice script, and I was shattered when after mentioning this plan to my mother on the 'phone, she said "*NO!*" She went on to explain that while she thought the idea excellent in theory, she simply would not hear of my going alone. I sighed. When my mother said no, my mother meant no. Dear, darling mother, I thought, what on earth do you imagine could possibly happen to me in Bournemouth that could not happen here in St. Athans or Leighton Buzzard or anywhere else for that matter.

She must have sensed that I was crushed, because after a pause she said one way around the problem would be for me to take my grandmother along. Granny badly needed a holiday, she continued, and I could take care of her. I was well aware that women of the world did not travel with their grandmothers, but I adored mine and leapt at the suggestion. Somehow she never seemed old to me. She had such vitality and zest for life, and loved young people. She was also tall and elegant, and had what I could only describe as "presence." She would enter a room and things seemed to happen—people immediately stood a little straighter, chairs would be pulled out, and the most comfortable place beside the fire would be offered. There was a lot to be said for travelling with my grandmother.

When the day of our departure arrived, Granny and I, kitted out to the wartime nines, left for Bournemouth from Waterloo station, both of us determined that the other should have the best of all possible holidays. My grandmother had been a widow for eight years, and although I think she was happy with us, I knew she must have suffered Saharas of loneliness without my grandfather. She, on the other hand, saw me beset by daily perils, and in need of spoiling.

The Royal Bath Hotel was sumptuous, and still retained a little of its pre-war grandeur. The staff, of course, had been drastically reduced, and instead of the rather lofty waiters of peacetime, there were some "dot and fetch it" old boys who had obviously known better days. Still they were very dignified and correct, doing their best to live up to the august surroundings. They directed a bevy of middle-aged waitresses, whom I suspect were graduates of Joe Lyon's Corner House chain. They, too, were extremely helpful and pleasant, and loved to engage my grandmother in long conversations about "the way things used to be."

We chose to sit in an alcove for dinner on our first evening. The napery was snowy and the pre-war crystal shone. There was even an orchestra of sorts, the players' mean age being about seventy. They ground out a sedate repertoire of Edwardian melodies, and I detected my grandmother's foot tapping and a dreamy expression on her face.

When we came in, I had also noticed a couple of young naval officers dining together on the far side of the restaurant. Before long, one of them worked his way over to our table, introduced himself, bowed to my grandmother, and asked me to dance. His name was John Marshall, and I offered up a special prayer of thanks to the gods of chance who had sent him my way. When he brought me back to our table, my grandmother looked up and said, "Young man, it's no good my sitting here alone, and your friend in the same predicament over there. Why don't you fetch him and come and join us?"

It was, of course, exactly what he had hoped for, and it took him roughly one second to collect his friend, Robert, and return to our table.

It was the beginning of a memorable week. We made an extremely compatible if rather unlikely foursome. After a late breakfast, we would "take the air," as my grandmother called it, along the esplanade. I would love to have walked on the sand, but the beaches were out of bounds, being mined and wired off. At the end of the seawall, we found a place that served fresh oysters. My grandmother would close her eyes in bliss as these succulent little morsels slipped down, assisted by a glass of champagne. It was a brief moment of gourmet madness and worth a thousand days of Spam.

In the afternoon, my grandmother would have a rest, and the three of us walked, explored, and poked in the shops that still had anything left to sell. By the end of the week, I had two naval officers swearing their undying love. I told them I loved them, too—as a sister—and that we would be friends forever. This was not exactly what they had in mind, but with my grandmother in attendance, and my own sturdy attempts to keep everything on a platonic footing, there was little either one of them could do except bow to the inevitable.

During our week at the Royal Bath, one of the other tables in the restaurant was occupied by a family comprising a mother, father, and a daughter who appeared nightly attired in her A.T.S. uniform. I had decided against wearing my uniform on the grounds that it was part of the holiday to get back into my civilian wardrobe. The entire family kept eyeing my rather "grande dame" grandmother and me with disapproval, particularly as I was obviously having a frivolous and perfectly lovely time. They were so transparently congratulating themselves that "at least some people's daughters know how to do their duty," that my grandmother pleaded with me to wear my uniform just once. I intended to, but only with full dramatic effect. I planned to make a stage entrance into the restaurant on our final evening in full W.A.A.F. fig, my two stripes blazing from my sleeve, and then sit back and lap up their reaction.

It was all I could have hoped for and more. We went down a little later than usual, to make sure we would be the last to arrive. The boys met us in the foyer, and I went in, spit and polish from head to toe, and flanked by two handsome naval lieutenants. The family in question was in conversation as we reached our table. Mamma looked up, gulped, and dug her husband violently in the ribs; he in turn nearly choked, and A.T.S. daughter turned in her chair, goggle-eyed and unbelieving. I smiled. It was a smile of pure and poisonous sweetness, and nodding my head graciously, I swept to my chair, followed by my grandmother, John, and Robert, each of whom in turn bestowed the same syrupy and spurious smile. In my mind, the curtain fell to tumultuous applause.

Blitzkrieg

THERE WAS a carousel quality about our life at Bentley Priory: on watch, off watch, eat, sleep, on watch again. Actually, sleep was of minimal importance and given the shortest shrift. When one is very young it is much more important to seek out excitement than to snooze away one's off-duty hours, and few of us turned down the opportunity to escape to London for an evening out.

We were paid next to nothing, but as dates were plentiful, it did not seem to matter too much. When we did have to pay our own way, we developed a series of stratagems to cut the cost of our outings. One such was to book a room for two, then smuggle in another two girls so we could split the tariff among four. We shared pillows, blankets, and took turns about the beds. There was a lot of diving for cover whenever the chambermaid knocked, although, looking back, I rather suspect the management knew what we were up to, and simply turned a wartime blind eye.

My close friendship with Liz continued, and we frequently went into London together. It was on one such occasion that we were having tea in the Strand Palace Hotel when the waiter presented us with a note, indicating two R.A.F. pilots at a nearby table as the source. Unfolding it, I read, "Hi, angel, I'm so lonely. May we come over and join you? Please don't say no."

I showed it to Liz, we glanced over, agreed they both looked "nice," and gave them a nod of assent. They were over in the proverbial trice and introduced themselves. The one who had written the note was called Bill Keough, and it turned out that he was one of the first Americans to cross into Canada and then make his way to England to join the R.A.F.

The cup of tea progressed into a full-scale date, with dinner followed by an evening at the theatre. The Luftwaffe was in full cry that night with bombs crashing all around us and everywhere the staccato blasts of the ack-ack guns. We scorned retreat into the shelters and, with youth's firm conviction in its own immortality, made our way to the theatre. When we emerged again it was to scenes of devastation, the pavements littered with shattered glass, fires burning, and buildings that had been standing a few hours ago, now just a mass of rubble. We saw a sad calvacade of stretchers being carried to the waiting ambulances and stopped to help when the overworked wardens asked for a hand in the digging. It did not seem real to me then, and does not now. I find, all these years later, that I cannot even begin to conjure up the magnitude of the horror.

I saw a lot of Bill after that evening. He was a charmer, attractively shy, with a lovely slow drawl that turned me to jelly, particularly when he called me "his angel." My mother loved him, and he spent most of his leaves at Warren Farm House. She would feed him American-style delicacies she received in food parcels from her family in Canada. Bill was such a happy person to be with that it seemed almost a contradiction in his personality when I uncovered his obsessively fatalistic streak. He knew, he said, that sooner or later he would be killed. I suppose this is a fear every combatant must know at some time or another, but with Bill it was different. He talked about it openly, as though it were an adventure toward which he was being irrevocably drawn.

I found I was becoming infected with this sense of inevitability, and so when my mother telephoned one sunlit spring morning, I knew before she told me that Bill had been killed. He had been shot down in a bombing raid over Kiel, my mother added, but I did not really hear her. I went into the loo, the only private spot on the base, and wept for Bill, who would never again call me "his angel," and whose life had been so overshadowed by death.

Only a few weeks later Liz received news that Philip, Bill's friend, had also been killed. This was the reality of war, tragic and personal, and no longer something remotely fought on a battle map. I found myself thinking more and more of Donald, and would hold the *D* on my chain very tightly and pray for his safety. If only I had some idea of his whereabouts, I thought miserably. Periodically, I would receive photostat letters from him, but there was never any clue as to where they had come from. When I wrote to him, I had to post the letters to the Admiralty for forwarding. I imagined him pacing an icy deck in the North Atlantic or, alternately, lolling on a beach in the South Pacific. In one letter he would write of his loneliness, and in the next he would enclose a programme of a risque review in New York. His life seemed to be a feast-or-famine affair, whereas mine was a continual excitement. I loved my work, and really felt that I was doing something of value. I had a crowded social life, and best of all, I had the enduring friendship of Liz.

One morning we were asked to report to the W.A.A.F. Commandant. We went in a little apprehensively and were genuinely flabbergasted when we were told that we had both been accepted for the Officer Cadet Training Unit and were scheduled to leave for Loughborough later in the summer.

"Liz, this is absolutely marvellous," I gloated after we left the Commandant's office. "I didn't think we would even be considered for at least another year."

Liz was not smiling as she said, "Do you realize, Moo, that this means we will have to go our separate ways? We've had such good times together, and I can't bear the thought of it ending, can you? Isn't it funny how good news is so often touched with sadness."

I had not thought it through, but Liz was right. After our training, it would mean our eventual separation. In a moment of high emotion, we made a pact, swearing to meet as often as possible, even if it involved one of us tearing down from the outer Hebrides and the other racing up from Land's End.

Gerry

M Y TWENTY-FIRST birthday was just over the horizon, and my parents were planning a dance in my honour. It was to be held at Warren Farm House, and the entire household was being thrown into a frenzy of preparation. There was a continual flow of correspondence back and forth and a fortune spent on telephone calls. I found it difficult to keep my mind on the sober duties of war with so many momentous decisions to be made on dress styles, guest lists, and other vital matters.

Not long before the planned party, I had met Gerry, a delightful Dutch naval commander serving in the British Navy. He was tall, with that special sort of scrubbed, Nordic good looks, and had impeccable manners. He was a few years older than I and had acquired a certain man-of-the-world polish. This, together with all his other assets and a wicked sense of humour, made him well-nigh irresistible. Within a few weeks of our first meeting, he had asked me to marry him. He was, he said, a man of quick decisions and knew his mind. Furthermore, he certainly knew how to pay court. I was deluged with flowers to such an embarrassing extent that I eventually shared them with the all-too-willing vicar of the local church. I am sure he cherished notions about my beautiful nature and generous heart, never knowing it was pure expediency. Whenever we met, Gerry had a charming and original present for me, and it was small wonder that my head turned at least a hundred degrees. It was really the first time that my love for Donald had been seriously put to the test. It was awful to find that memories of Donald were beginning to fade. Eternal love is difficult for the young, particularly after a two years' absence, and particularly when one is being so assiduously wooed by another.

Gerry had promised to come to my twenty-first if he could arrange his leave. Apart from the pleasure of having him there, I looked on him as a major social asset because of his skill at the piano. He loved to play, and to my unbiased ears sounded just like another Oscar Peterson. Once at the piano, he was quite happy to play all night if necessary.

The day of the party finally arrived— the thirteenth of June, 1942. I dashed off to Harrod's to pick up my dress, a blissful creation in red patterned silk, with a three-tiered, accordion-pleated skirt, edged in white. This was followed by a trip to the hairdresser's, and a few other last minute commissions before I finally caught a train for home.

Friends and relations were already arriving at the station, with my father and our cowman, Bill, acting as chauffeurs. In addition to a fairly fulsome complement of family and neighbours, there were to be about fifty other guests at the party. I had a qualm or two about Donald's not being there for this landmark occasion, but this disappointment was balanced off against the obvious difficulties of having both Donald and Gerry at the same party. Elaborate arrangements had been made for putting up out-of-towners, like my childhood friend Catherine, who had come down from her A.T.S. station in Northern Ireland for the event. Our bedrooms, already bulging with wartime billets, were turned into dormitories and (never ask me how) as many as fourteen were wedged into one room. Even the summer house at the end of the garden was pressed into service, allocated to my father and three naval officers.

It was a beautiful, warm evening and the dance was well underway. As soon as Gerry arrived, I thought, everything will be perfect. I then happened to glance across the room and saw my parents standing together. Despite war, shortages, cramped space, and a multitude of problems, they had managed to give their first-born this gift of a party. I loved them so much, and impulsively left my partner and darted across the room to tell them so.

Midway through the party the 'phone rang. It was Gerry. He could not make it. I was bitterly disappointed as I had so much wanted to welcome him into my own world, out of uniform, and surrounded by my family. I battled against a let-down feeling, and suddenly wished that the ancient friend of my grandmother's who was picking out "The Blue Danube" and "Tea for Two" on the piano would get with it.

Around midnight, when I was convinced the party was beginning to flag, I saw my mother moving through the hall, asking as she went if anyone had heard the doorbell. Suddenly the miracle was there—Gerry, his arms full of flowers, and a grin splitting his face.

From then on, the evening was back in the groove. The old gentleman was relieved of his duties at the piano. Gerry took over and things were soon back in full swing. We seemed to dance forever. As a matter of fact, at one point my father was seen searching for a torch, feeling it was probably time to escort the naval officers back to the summer house. He was more than a bit taken aback to find upon drawing the blackout curtains that it was broad daylight and the June sun was already quite high. The party flowed out onto the garden and might have begun all over again had we not been called in for a breakfast of bacon and eggs.

By 10 a.m., things had quietened down, and Gerry and I found ourselves alone for the first time. The day was warm and sunny, and after walking in the garden, we sat down under the old Victoria plum tree near the house. After a minute or two, Gerry gently put his arms around me and asked me to marry him.

I was in a welter of emotions. I thought I loved him—was even sure that I did—yet at the same time I knew I was not ready for marriage. I had seen so many lonely young wives, left out of so many things and growing more and more restless. No, I definitely did not want to be married, nor did I want to lose Gerry. I had to manage to get my feelings across and still our relationship alive. I took a deep breath and tried to explain. He kept interrupting, but I made him let me finish. He was silent for awhile, and then he grinned his soul-restoring grin.

"All right, you win," he said, "but only for six months, then I'll ask you again, and I promise you right now that I won't take no for an answer."

I smiled, relieved. In six months' time, who knows, I might be ready to marry, but in the meantime I had escaped commitment without sending Gerry out of my life forever.

*   *   *

It would have seemed a bit of an anti-climax after the feverish excitement of my party, to say nothing of a proposal of marriage, but we were so busy in the "Ops Room" that there was little time to think of anything else. The enemy had stepped up their bombing raids: London was a holocaust, Coventry devastated, and still the war dragged on. It brought its tragedies. My mother telephoned one day with the sad news that two of our nearest neighbours had each lost sons, and that a third friend had been taken prisoner by the Germans. These were boys with whom I had played tennis, ridden, and danced a thousand years ago in that seemingly endless summer before the war. My mood was indigo, and I felt suddenly old in knowledge and grief.

On the first day of July, I returned to my billet after watch to see a telegram in my locker. It was from the Admiralty. I began to crumble inside, as though everything that held me together had come loose, and I held the wire for a long time before I could open it. Oh please, God, don't let it be Donald, I prayed. Donald, who had been my most cherished friend and whom I had shamefully and resolutely relegated to the back of my mind. Finally, I tore the flap and pulled out the message: "The Admiralty regrets to inform you . . . " I could read no further than the name. For some reason I had never thought it could be Gerry. No one with such an appetite for life, and such joy in it, could possibly be dead. I felt strangely still and frozen, until the release of tears finally came. I slipped down beside my bed, and wept once more for those who would never come back to fulfill the promise of lives that had barely begun.

I did not hear the door open and was not aware that Liz had come in until I turned and saw her there, her face ravaged and her eyes full of tears.

"Oh Liz," I said, "what's wrong?"

She sank to the floor beside me and buried her head on my shoulder, sobbing. She was crying so hard, I found it difficult to catch what she was saying.

"It's my brother, Tom," she cried, "he's missing . . . shot down yesterday . . . somewhere over Germany. Oh, Moo, I can't believe this is happening . . . I love him so much . . . this bloody, bloody war! Poor Mum . . . Dad's away somewhere at sea, and she's had to take this news on her own. I've got to go home . . . can you help me arrange it?"

I tried to pull myself together, and decided not to tell Liz about Gerry just then. She had not noticed my own tears, and I felt she had enough to contend with as it was. A brother, I thought, must be a very special relationship. I had always envied girls with brothers, and I felt the sharpness of my friend's loss. God, how I was beginning to hate this war.

We were both granted compassionate leave, and I went home with Liz. I did not go into the house with her, for I felt that she and her mother would want to be alone. We kissed good-bye and I caught a train to Guildford.

My mother seemed alarmed to see how pale I looked as I walked through the door. "Darling," she exclaimed, "whatever is the matter?" I could not answer but just threw myself into her arms and sobbed out my news. There were no words to ease the pain, so intuitively she just held me and stroked my hair as she had done so many times when

I was a child.

When I finally managed to compose myself a little, I turned to my mother and said forlornly, "Oh Mummy, what am I going to do. I feel so lost. Everyone I come to care for seems to get himself killed, and the war just goes on and on. I'm not sure I can take it any more."

My mother just lifted her shoulders helplessly. During her nursing days, she had seen death, the horrors of mutilation, grief, and pain enough to last a lifetime. She would have protected me from all this if she could, but in war there is no immunity, and all she could do was reach out and hold my hand in silent understanding.

Foothills of Olympus

A FEW WEEKS later, Liz and I travelled together to Loughborough to begin our Officers' Training programme in the Officer Cadet Training Unit (or O.C.T.U.). Far from the uncertainty of our arrival at Leighton Buzzard, this time we approached our new post poised and confident, stripes on our sleeves, and ready to hold our own with anyone.

The course was to last a month, and involved a work-packed schedule. It was another challenge we both enjoyed, and we were determined to do well. I have to admit that the thought of becoming an officer was pretty heady. I had always looked on them as being just a notch or two below God, and here I was standing in the foothills of Mount Olympus. What I did not realize was that in gaining the heights, I would be losing, at least to some extent, the relaxed camaraderie of life among the "other ranks."

Most of the women in the higher echelons of command were older. Many were spinsters who had found in the war something which at last gave purpose to their lives. To me it seemed their own position, and the general pecking order was so important to them that a plethora of petty jealousies frequently distorted their judgment. There seemed to be resentment against young officers coming up, particularly if they happened to be pretty. It was as though they regarded the privileges of rank almost as compensation for having missed out in other directions. On this basis, they could, I suppose, have seen it as somehow unfair that girls who already had the advantages of youth and good looks should also receive officer status. Yet it was true that the only sort of girl this type of officer seemed to be able to tolerate was either the bespectacled little mouse or the strident anti-man feminist.

At first, I was rather taken aback when having done nothing to blot my copybook, I found myself confronting tight lips and suspicious glares. Once again, I breathed a prayer of gratitude for my schooling and its lessons in adjusting to life in a female community. I decided the only course open to me was to go ahead and do my job, and ignore any hostility.

They were not all like that, of course. We were billeted in a semi-detached house in Loughborough with an absolutely delightful W.A.A.F. officer in charge. She did much to create the atmosphere that existed in the house, which was pretty crowded and could have produced a lot of tension and frayed nerves. Instead, everyone seemed to slot in nicely. We were all ambitious and spurred one another on, knowing that the better we did at O.C.T.U., the better the chances of future promotion.

Drilling was a daily occurrence, and there is no question about it that we became very good. When we marched through Loughborough, every arm swinging in unison, we were conscious of the admiration of the crowd, and would not have been human if we had not felt rather proud of ourselves. I passionately hoped that whatever role my officer training would bring me to, it would involve drill. The thought of starting off with a raggle-taggle collection of females and bringing them up to the same high standard we had attained was something I felt I could really get my teeth into.

One day we were told that Cecil Beaton, the famous photographer, was coming to Loughborough to do a series of photographs on life at the O.C.T.U.— the W.A.A.F. at work and play, or some such theme. They were to be used for a main feature in *Picture Post Magazine*, and naturally everyone was keen as mustard to get in on the act.

The only things I had ever seen of Cecil Beaton's work

were dreamy, soft-focus shots of royalty posing beside Palace roses, or debutantes in oceans of white tulle parading in front of an improbable background of Grecian pillars. What could he do to romanticize all that blue serge, starched shirts and lisle stockings! Whatever he was thinking privately, he approached the project as though it were a society garden party. He appeared in a cream-coloured suit with a rather flamboyant silk hanky spilling out of his pocket, and snapped away happily. He would look knowingly into the lens, then direct us into all sorts of different poses.

At one point, he requested that we should do a drilling routine on the parade ground. Obligingly the W.A.A.F. officer put us through our paces, finally bringing the squad to a halt and ordering us to stand at ease.

"That was divine, darling," Mr. Beaton beamed, turning to the officer. "Now do you think we could get the dear young things to drape their arms sideways onto the next girl's shoulder?"

The sturdy officer, who must have weighed in around thirteen stone, swung on him, bellowing out with such force that it nearly blew the frail Mr. Beaton into the air, silk kerchief and all. "Do you mean Command Right Dress?"

"Well . . . yes . . . if you say that's it, duckie," he replied with an eloquent shrug and a wave of his hand. "It sounded *something* like that."

I came to the conclusion that the reason he was a truly great photographer with such an intuitive feel for dramatic effect was that he was also a born actor. He knew he was delighting us and confounding our officer, and he played the role to the hilt.

The month sped by, and once more the results were posted up on the notice board. I was afraid to look and had to resort to getting Liz to relay the results.

"Oh, Moo," she burst out, "you've outdone yourself. You've passed with distinction— 96 percent."

I was ecstatic and dashed off to the nearest telephone to

tell my parents the good news. My father was at home and answered my call.

"Oh, well done! Very, very well done, my dear," he said when I told him, barely able to contain the pride in his voice. "Hold on, old thing, I'll fetch your mother."

I could hear the excited babble in the background, exclamations of delight, paeans of praise, and everyone talking at once. My parents' obvious joy in my achievement was reward in itself. I was their first-born, the one in whom they had put their early hopes, and for me to do well was to give substance to their dreams. I put the icing on the cake when I told them I was also getting two weeks' leave, that I would be home in time for dinner, and would they kindly prepare a fatted calf.

Rustle in the Wheat

G OING HOME for me was rather like the medieval refugee making it to the door of the church and calling out
"sanctuary." Home meant a retreat to normalcy, the quiet
of the fields and the hills and, not to be underestimated,
the bliss of soft beds and deep, long baths. As the war intensified, however, I found there was little enough sanctuary anywhere, not even at Warren Farm House.

Still, no one could imagine how I anticipated those two
weeks' leave in the peace of the countryside. Shortly after
arriving home, I made my duty rounds in the neighbourhood—Donald's parents and, of course, the "Sisters."
The Sisters were our nearest neighbours and lived in a
wonderful old house that had stayed suspended in time
with the death of Queen Victoria. Both ladies were spinsters, and absolutely delightful. They affected a rather
archaic mode of dress, being much given to Bertha collars,
high-necked "morning dresses," and cameos. As a child, I
knew I could always count on a bang-up tea at the Sisters,
and consequently never had to be coerced into a visit.

As their house was spacious, they had not escaped the
billeting officer and were presently playing hostess to a
pretty young mother from London's East End and her two
small children. Her husband, Joseph Cuthbert, was a
docker and often worked around the clock, but whenever
he could he would try to get down to visit his family. While
he would always be welcomed in for a meal, he ran into
solid granite when it came to staying the night. The Sisters
were sorry, but they simply could not have it. As a result,

my mother dug up yet another camp bed from somewhere and fashioned the poor man a miniscule hidey-hole in our house. As a matter of fact, there were so many comings and goings at the farm that I never knew who would be in residence when I came home.

The weather for my leave was glorious, growing warmer with each passing day until we were actually in the middle of a totally un-English heat wave. On this particular day, I remember, it had been desperately hot, and after our evening meal, my mother, Nellie, Flo and I were sitting outdoors to cool off and enjoy the fragrance of the summer evening. The landscape of the farm had changed somewhat with the war. On a directive from the Department of Agriculture, my father had three fields put into wheat. It was high now, and a source of great pride to my father whenever he was home to enjoy it. He was not with us this weekend, nor was anyone else except for the aforementioned Mr. Cuthbert, who had arrived from London earlier in the day. He had taken his wife out for the evening and had not yet returned, so the four of us sat for a long time and watched the moon rise, flooding the fields.

It was a still, breathless night, interrupted suddenly by what sounded like rustling in the night. It must be some animal, I thought, until Flo said, in a rather nervous whisper, that she thought she heard the sound of voices.

"Don't be silly," my mother said, "who on earth would be in the wheat fields at this hour."

She stopped, and we all looked at each other, the horror unspoken. *Germans!* We were always being alerted about a parachute invasion, or sneak drops, or pilots bailing out. Flo was busy explaining in a loud stage whisper to Nellie, who, once the information was digested, looked distractedly at my mother.

"Whatever shall we do, Madam? They're vicious, that's what they are!" Then as an even more horrifying thought struck her, she exclaimed, "Here, what if they get into my larder?"

Trust Nellie, I thought, to get her priorities right.

"Now let's not jump to any conclusions before we investigate," my mother announced. "There could be a perfectly rational explanation. Muriel, you fetch me the torch from the hook inside the door, then the three of you go indoors and wait for me while I go and see what's there."

That there was *something* out there was no longer in doubt. We could see the wheat moving in the moonlight, and there were definitely sounds. Everyone protested that Mother simply could not go in there alone. Although I was firmly convinced that my mother could take on the whole German army, if necessary, I also knew I could never face my father (or myself for that matter) if I let her go alone. Finally we agreed that Nellie and Flo would go inside, and if we signalled them with three quick flashes from the torch, they were to 'phone the police or the Home Guard or Winston Churchill or *somebody* instantly. One of them was to stay by the telephone; the other to be ready with a meat cleaver or whatever lethal weapon came to hand.

All this strategy having been worked out, Mother and I moved stealthily toward the wheat field. The sounds had come from the far side, some distance from the house, and we agreed not to use the torch until the last moment. The moon was almost full, and there was enough light to see our way. Mother insisted that I stay behind her, although I personally rather fancied a flanking attack or a pincer movement.

It was eerie creeping through the long rows of wheat, their delicate feathery tops barely moving in the still night. We were very quiet and could hear the sound closer now, almost more like a flailing about than a rustle. At this moment, my mother put her fingers to her lips, raised her torch, and shone it directly into the wheat at the source of the disturbance.

I can only remember the briefest glimpse of tangled bodies, disarrayed clothing and two white, startled faces staring up at us, before my mother quickly turned off the torch.

"Who is it?" I hissed.

My mother drew a deep breath as she turned toward me, silently waving her torch to indicate that I move along as fast as was humanly possible. When we got out of earshot, she pulled me aside. "Muriel, my dear, not a word to any-one—it was simply poor Mr. Cuthbert escorting his wife back to the Sisters. They had stopped for a *rest*," she added firmly, stressing the last word.

I said nothing but secretly hugged that word "escorting." I was, perhaps, a trifle naive, but not that naive, and I could equally have hugged my mother for her brave at-tempt to preserve my girlish innocence. I could not blame the poor man, being allowed no connubial access at the Sisters, and only a camp bed in a corner at the Farm. Ah, well, I thought, as we returned to the house, if it is true that love will find a way, there could be less romantic places than in the middle of a moon-drenched wheat field on a beautiful night in high summer.

Balloons of
Pucklechurch

BACK FROM the excitement of my leave, I reluctantly left for my new posting at R.A.F. Station Pucklechurch, near Bristol. I was terribly disappointed at this appointment. Most of my friends were being sent to well-known fighter stations or Bomber Command. Liz was thrilled at going to a bomber station in Lincolnshire, and here I was being exiled to this godforsaken spot of which no one I knew had ever heard. To make matters worse, it was Balloon Command, of all things. They assured me it was vital work, and involved the flying and maintenance of the barrage balloons, which covered all major cities to protect them from low-flying enemy aircraft. Heaving a resigned sigh, I accepted the inevitable with as much grace as I could muster, and promised myself that I would apply to be posted back to Fighter Command as soon as I decently could.

Liz and I met in London for our last dinner, a sort of "farewell to ourselves," and it was an emotional parting. We were two different people from the girls who had larked about, bashing in cap peaks, and meeting strange young officers under the clock at Waterloo. Our shared tragedies which had taken so much from our lives conversely added so much to our feeling for one another. Liz had been the best possible friend, and I knew I would never find a better.

I missed her acutely as the train sped toward Bristol. I felt apprehensive. It would have been so different if Liz and I were going to this new post together. Pucklechurch! What a name! I philosophized away to myself about one door closing and another opening, and how the best was yet to be and all the other bolstering cliches that I could dredge up, but I was still feeling very much the new girl when the train pulled into Bristol.

I set about trying to find a bus to Pucklechurch. "To where?" said an elderly porter. "Never heard of it. Why don't you ask that cab driver over there."

Much to my relief, he at least knew of it, so I got in and eventually was duly deposited at the guard room. I signed in, and a pleasant N.C.O. escorted me to the Officer's Mess. She saluted and left me alone in the entrance. Almost immediately I was approached by a middle-aged W.A.A.F. flight officer. She was not smiling, and I sensed what today's young would call "negative vibes." I saluted smartly, and the salute was returned in a half-hearted fashion.

"You are Assistant Section Officer Gane, I presume?"

"Yes, ma'am," I replied, feeling the chill.

"Well, remove your cap and follow me. I suppose you want a cup of tea?" she inquired grudgingly.

"That would be very nice, thank you, ma'am," I replied.

Her cold eyes appraised me from head to toe, taking in every minute detail. It was totally unnerving, and to my shame, I began to feel the corners of my lips quivering and the sting of tears. Do not give her the satisfaction, I told myself furiously. Here I was with all the enthusiasm in the world, dying to give of my best for the greater glory of Pucklechurch, and here was this harridan undermining me before I even started.

"You will find your fellow officers are, for the most part, a good deal older than you, and I would strongly advise you to follow their lead closely to avoid making any unnecessary mistakes. We demand an extremely high standard at Pucklechurch, and there is no room for officers who do not pull their weight. You will find your quarters in the second hut on the right. I shall expect to see you present in the

Mess at seven o'clock," she concluded, turning on her heel and striding out.

Well! There's a heart I haven't won, I thought to myself, as I made a face at her retreating back. I gathered up my luggage, alternating between feeling forlorn and angry. She is not going to grind me down, I told myself, as I trudged over to my hut and went along the corridor, looking for No. 13. At least that was a good omen. I had been born on Friday, the thirteenth of June, and the number meant good luck to me. The door was at the far end of the corridor, so I knocked cautiously and waited. There was no reply, so I turned the handle and rather tentatively peered in. I was pleasantly surprised to find a bright little room, with two beds and overlooking an open area. The view was not exactly a landscape painting, but at least it was green, and there were no buildings in sight. I started to unpack and put out the photographs that went with me everywhere: my parents, sisters, my home, and the entire animal kingdom of Warren Farm House. There now, I thought, I have marked off my territory, and no matter what happens in the course of the day, I always have this as my place to come back to.

I heard voices along the corridor. The door to our bedroom opened and in came a young officer.

"Oh, hello, you've arrived, I see. My name is Mary White, and I am sorry not to have been on hand to welcome you. We thought you would be coming later."

She is nice at any rate, I thought. I smiled and we shook hands.

"By the way, whom did you see?" she asked.

"I don't know her name," I replied, "she never mentioned it. Oh, sorry," I added as an afterthought, "I'm Muriel Gane."

"What did she look like?" Mary persisted. "Was she a crusty old bitch?"

I had no intention of falling into a trap, so I replied warily. "Well, I don't know about that. She was not as young as you and I, and seemed a bit severe."

"Yes, that's her all right. I'm sorry to seem to be interrogating you, but I feel it is only fair to put you in the picture. She is absolutely venomous, and really knows how to wield the whip. She, and two others just like her, are always waiting to pounce. The only people under forty are Suzy and myself. Even the R.A.F. officers are the same age as our fathers. The sad thing is they act like schoolboys let out at recess, and expect us to fall all over them. The only really decent place in the whole camp is the Sergeants' Mess. We can relax there and have fun with people our own age. It upsets the officers, though, that we spend more of our free time there than in our own dreary Mess."

She chattered on as I completed my unpacking and told me about Suzy. Suzy was petite, very pretty, and had become a war widow the day before her twenty-first birthday. How awful, I thought, my mind flashing back to Gerry, and the afternoon under the plum tree in our garden. If I had accepted him, I, too, would have been a twenty-one-year-old widow, with my life adrift. I tried not to think of Gerry, blotting out the picture of him standing in our doorway with his arms full of flowers.

I changed my shirt, and together with Mary, headed towards the Mess, reaching it just before seven. As we entered, conversations petered out, and I was aware that we were being watched curiously as we crossed the room. I just wished they would carry on talking so that I would feel less like a particularly loathsome specimen under a microscope. Mary led me up to the officer I had met that afternoon, who was now flanked by two other equally formidable types. They looked like three birds of prey, lined up and waiting for the kill. I mustered up every bit of self-confidence I could, and politely introduced myself to the other two.

I did not have time to assess their reactions because at that moment the Station Commander came up and made himself known. He was about my father's age, but with a natural charm and kindliness, and immediately put me at ease. I detected a flash of annoyance on the faces of the three, and not without some satisfaction moved on with the Station Commander for further introduction.

Word soon got around camp that a new W.A.A.F officer had arrived, and as Mary had predicted, we were invited to the Sergeants' Mess the following evening.

They were holding an informal dance, and a very good-looking flight sergeant headed over in my direction and asked me to dance. He was unusually tall, and I remember thinking how nice it was to dance with someone who did not stop at my shoulder. I was five foot nine, and if I had any sort of heels on, it was difficult to find a partner I could look up to. His name was Bill, and he was the Physical Training Instructor. As this was also to be my role for the W.A.A.F. on the station, I was sure we would be seeing a lot of each other.

I found the next day that I was fortunate in that my work took me away from the "Three Musketeers," as we dubbed the trio of senior officers. Not so poor Mary and Suzy, who worked in the same office block and who regaled me every evening with tales of their petty tyrannies.

Even so, I had to admit it was a well-run station, and new ideas and experiments were always being carried out to try to achieve total efficiency. One of the problems the camp faced was overcrowding in the dining hall. The personnel were spending too long over meals, relaxing and gossiping instead of vacating their seats and allowing the next contingent of diners to come in.

A senior R.A.F. officer hit upon what he considered a brilliant scheme. The men and women would be segregated and each group allowed twenty-five minutes for a meal. The arrangement was that one group would go first one day and the other first the next day, and so on. In order that there would be no misunderstanding, a light would go on over the dining hall door— blue for the airmen and red for the girls. It all sound fairly straightforward until the practice run on the day I was duty officer. The W.A.A.F. had been selected to go in second, and we were hanging about patiently waiting for the blue bulb to go out and the red to come on. When it finally did, I led the girls into the vast hall only to be greeted by deafening cat calls, wolf whistles, and a considerable repertoire of bawdy comments. At first we could not understand what they were going on about, then the penny dropped. It was that blasted red light! Why could it not have been green, yellow, orange, anything but red, which my face now matched in colour. The incident became sort of a station joke, and for some time I was nicknamed "Madame" and solicitous inquiries were made after "my girls."

I had been seeing Bill, the P.T. instructor, quite often, and that same evening he had invited me to go out with him to a little pub somewhere in the back of beyond, about a three-mile walk from the station. The problem that we were both well aware of was that officers were not to be seen in the company of other ranks, unless wearing civvies. We arranged to meet after dark, well away from the station gates. It was a cold and frosty night in mid-November, but there was a pale winter moon and a sort of magic about the evening that I remember still. We walked down the country road as the snow crunched under our feet, and the odd owl hooted from the dark shadows of the trees.

Bill was well known in the pub, and we were welcomed in beside a blazing fire and given hot toddies. We had such a truly happy evening that I was surprised by Bill's sudden change of mood on the walk back. He had become very silent, and when I asked him why, he passed it off with some facile compliment about wondering how he could be so lucky as to have found such a gorgeous girl in Pucklechurch of all places. What he left unsaid, however, was what he was really wondering, namely whether to tell me that he was married. In all the weeks we had been seeing each other, it had never occurred to me that he might be.

It was a thoroughly unpleasant shock, therefore, when I returned to my room a few days later to find a letter from Bill on my chest of drawers. Its import was that he had asked for compassionate leave, as his wife had been rushed to the hospital with an acute appendix and he did not want me to hear this news from anyone else. My emotions ranged the gamut: outrage at Bill's deception; anger at myself for being so naive; and finally a kind of understanding. The war made everything so unreal. He was lonely and far from home; our relationship had never developed into anything serious; and the chances of his wife's ever knowing that he was squiring someone else about were very remote. It was true that had I known he was married, I would not have gone out with him in the first place, but I could not really bring myself to censure him too severely.

This charitable conclusion, however, was not the end of the matter. The following morning, I was told to report to my senior W.A.A.F. officer. She was waiting for me with what I can only describe as an expression of ill-concealed triumph— rather like someone who has patiently baited a trap and finally seen it sprung. It had come to her attention, she began, that I had been "keeping company" with an N.C.O. Once launched, she went on and on through the most almighty dressing down I had ever received. Her voice rose to a crescendo as she described the infamy of one of "her girls" cavorting about with an N.C.O. I could not have been in deeper disgrace if I had taken up with an enemy agent.

Throughout her diatribe, however, I did see that she had a certain amount of sense on her side, and began to realize that I had been a bit of an idiot. There was also a good possibility of an adverse report coming up. Well, I thought, what is done is done. The most sensible thing to do now would be to apply for a re-posting. I had never really been happy at Pucklechurch and did not particularly enjoy the work. A lot of what I was learning involved the intricacies of flying balloons, mastering the art of tying knots, splicing wire and winching balloons up into the heavens. At least I had Bill to thank for helping me make my decision to apply for a new posting, and returning to my billet I sat down and wrote out the application.

A Lucky Break

M Y GRANDMOTHER had a vast collection of "wise sayings," and one of her favorites was, "If the tide goes out, it must also come in." It is amazing how often truisms turn out to be true. I had barely dried my tears over the ebbing of my fortunes when I found myself being swept back on an unexpected floodtide.

It began on that same evening when we were scheduled to play a match of mixed officers against mixed sergeants. The game was a sort of no-holds-barred netball, and took place in one of the large hangars. It was a rough game to begin with and was made even rougher by the fact that it was played on a concrete floor.

I suspect I was still dwelling on the troubles of the day, and that I was not really concentrating on the game in hand, because all I remember was taking a mammoth leap into the air to catch a ball and colliding with our station warrant officer, a giant of a Scotsman. There was a clash like cymbals, the sensation of flying, then a bone-wrenching thud, followed by an excruciating pain in my wrist. I picked myself up before anyone could reach my side, protesting rather dizzily that I was absolutely, perfectly fine. No, no difficulty at all. Of course I could go on with the game. I sometimes wonder if I will say "fine, thank you" on my deathbed. The truth of the matter was that I was far from fine, but I hate fuss, and besides we were almost at the end of the game, and we were winning! I had already scored four of our six goals, and was not going to be cheated of the plaudits of the crowd by being borne ignominiously off the floor. So I managed to hang on while a large angular lump developed, and my whole arm throbbed agonizingly.

At the end of the game, I was rewarded by ringing cheers and thumps on the back. However, when it came to pumping my hand, it was observed that it hung at right angles to my arm, and I was scurried off to my room where the poor misshapen thing was gently lowered into a washbasin of cold water. As it continued to swell, there was nothing for it but to make my way down to the R.A.F. nursing sister and hope she would be in her room. Luckily for me, she was, and inspected my wrist with growing concern. "My dear, you've broken it . . . badly I would guess. I'll bandage it up with some splints which should help, but you will have to go to hospital tomorrow to see the extent of the damage. I'll make arrangements and let you know."

Although she gave me some aspirin, I am afraid poor Mary did not get much sleep that night. I was in agony, and tossed and turned incessantly. Dressing the next morning was a problem, and without Mary's help I doubt if I could have managed. We crossed over to the Mess for breakfast, where I was clucked over sympathetically by everyone except the "Three Musketeers," who doggedly munched away in a corner, determined not to notice my plight.

Sister came to find me to give me my instructions. I was to go to the Naval Hospital at Barrow Gurney near Bristol. There would be an R.A.F. vehicle to take me there and bring me back, and wishing me luck, she wafted away looking lovely and comforting in her starched whites and crisp veil.

I was duly picked up and driven the twenty-five miles to the hospital. It was early December, and a pale, winter sun was doing its best to cheer me up. As we turned into the long driveway leading up to the hospital, the surroundings were so beautiful that I could not help but feel better. The lawns stretched out to the edge of thick woodlands, and I caught the sight of pheasants and deer among the ferns. What a place to recuperate, I thought, as I made my way into the hospital waiting room. After what seemed an interminable time of shifting about and looking at old magazines, I was finally ushered into the doctor's room. He looked up from his desk as I entered.

Never let anyone tell you that there is no such thing as human chemistry. You might as well claim that a light does not go on when you pull a switch. I knew that something magical was happening when our eyes met. It was like touching someone and getting an electric shock. For a moment I forgot all about the reason for my being there. There was a funny little silence, and then he said, "Hello, it's Muriel, isn't it," looking down at his notes, "and what have you been up to?"

I felt suddenly a little shy. "Well, I think I have broken my wrist . . . last night . . . in a match . . . it was sort of a netball . . . and the floor was concrete . . . and . . . "

"Good heavens," he interrupted, "what was a pretty girl like you doing in a game like that?"

"Oh, it's quite all right normally, but last night I collided with a gigantic Scot, and I wanted to keep on playing because we were winning . . ." I wound down, thinking how stupid it all suddenly sounded.

"Well, you've got guts, I'll say that for you, but you also have an extremely nasty fracture," he said, removing the splints and gently feeling my wrist.

The pain was awful with the splint removed, and I hated myself for not being able to hold back the tears. He nobly pretended not to notice and added, "We'll have this x-rayed for you, and when I have put a plaster cast on it, you won't even feel it, I can promise you."

When he finished plastering me from my fingers up to my elbow, I found he was quite right. There was no pain whatever. I smiled and thanked him.

"You've been marvellous, Muriel—may I call you Muriel? Now then, I suggest that I take you into the Mess for a drink and some lunch. You certainly deserve it. Besides, I want to learn a great deal more about you. Incidentally," he went on, "I've sent your driver away until 3:30 this afternoon, and so there is no point in your trying to do a Cinderella on me, as your pumpkin won't return until then."

I was delighted, but even if I had not been, there was something about this handsome, blonde six-footer that swept people along in the direction he would have them go. We went into the Mess, and although there were a lot of greetings such as "Robin— over here, old man," he carefully guided me to a table set off by itself. We had barely sat down when we were joined by another naval officer, who immediately challenged Robin. "Well, here you are— do you realize I have been waiting for you all morning? What on earth have you been up to?"

Robin laughed and turned his hand palm upward in my direction. "This is what I have been up to all morning. Peter, may I introduce Muriel, who has a particularly nasty fracture, and a particularly charming personality. Don't be put off by my bumptious friend," he added in a loud aside to me. "He really is quite a decent type."

Lunch was over and 3:30 p.m. arrived much too quickly, but not before we had arranged another meeting for the next Saturday. I had told them about Suzy and how pretty she was and how lonely she had been, and Peter was enthusiastic about making it a foursome.

Robin led me over to the waiting R.A.F. vehicle and helped me in as though I were some rare and fragile thing too precious to be left to chance. Not since Gerry had I known such attention. I felt suddenly very feminine and in need of protection, despite the tailored uniform, the no-nonsense stockings, and a positive armload of plaster in the shape of a truncheon. As Robin closed the door of the car, he said he would write to my medical officer and inform him that it would be necessary for me to come into Barrow Gurney once a week until the cast was ready to be removed. I was delighted at the prospect but could not help but wonder about using broken wrists to further Love's own purpose.

*   *   *

Coping with that terrible plaster cast proved more of a trial than almost anything I had yet encountered in my Air Force career. The trouble was that I am left-handed and it was my left wrist that I had broken, so everything I did seemed doubly awkward. Trying to do my hair was an exercise in futility, as it was almost impossible to push in hair clips. To make matters worse, W.A.A.F. regulations clearly stated that not one whisper of hair must be allowed to touch the collar. After a lot of struggling, I finally got it down to a fine art. I would place the full length of the cast against the back of my hair, and then proceed to push a clip in alongside it.

Only once did this technique let me down. A senior W.A.A.F. officer was visiting Pucklechurch and her searching eyes detected a strand of hair on the collar of one of her W.A.A.F. officers. My station officer, however, did not immediately leap to my defence. Instead, she practically rubbed her hands in glee at my having been singled out, and later took great pleasure in chastising me further in front of my fellow officers. She certainly was a sweetheart!

However, life has its compensations and Saturday came at last. I took extra care in getting ready. I pressed my uniform, wound my hair around a black ribbon, leaving a fetching little bit peeking out, and put on grey silk stockings rather than the regulation lisle. I sprayed myself lavishly with "L'heure Bleu," the gift of an erstwhile boyfriend who said he had selected it because it was the way he was feeling when he did not get a letter from me.

I was glad that I had been able to persuade Suzy to come with me. She had had a rotten time since her husband had been killed, and I wanted her to feel happy again, if only for an evening.

Robin and Peter duly arrived and we took them into our

Mess for a drink. Officers from the Senior Service were a bit of a rarity in our Mess, but I introduced them to everybody I knew, including the Station Commander. When we left I was amused to hear the sudden babble of conversation.

The men had chosen to take us to a little club in Bristol. The lights were dim and the tables candlelit, but the dance floor was the size of a pocket hankie. Somewhere in a far corner, a small trio was playing all the wonderful, sentimental music of the period—"Two Sleepy People," "I'll Be Seeing You," and "Cheek to Cheek." The dance floor being what it was, we found ourselves just swaying to the rhythm, and moving only if space permitted. The trio swung into "I'm in the Mood for Love," and it was as though the words had just come from the lyricist's pen that very moment and were meant for us alone.

The music stopped and we broke away. We did not say anything, but we reached for each other's hand and I knew that this time it was Love, heavily capitalized and the Real Thing.

We wandered back to our table, hand-in-hand, to find Suzy and Peter deep in conversation. I was then, and still am, a terminal romantic. I desperately wanted things to turn out well for them: I wanted Suzy to find in Peter a "second Spring," and I wanted them to live happily ever after.

As it transpired, I was not all that far off the mark. Peter and Suzy were only too happy to fit into my romantic concept of them, and the four of us met almost every weekend. In addition to these pre-arranged dates, I had the overwhelming plus of my weekly medical visits. After a cursory pat of my cast, Robin and I would have lunch and then take a long walk in the glorious woods surrounding the hospital. My life came into balance again—the frustrations of Pucklechurch being compensated for by the happiness of Bristol.

Weeks after my accident, Robin announced that much as he loved my coming to Bristol every Tuesday, his medical conscience was beginning to bother him. "You know, Moo," he said, "if we leave that cast on much longer, I doubt whether you will have any arm left inside it. There is nothing for it but to take it off and have a look see."

The plaster was by now a pretty sorry sight. It was crumbling at the edges, dirty, and covered with graffiti, so much so that I had been forced to cover it with a chopped-off grey lisle stocking. Slowly, and with infinite gentleness, Robin cut away the plaster until it finally fell to the floor in a heap of limp crumbs. There, revealed for all to see, was a thin, wasted, dried-up little arm, the skin looking like an ancient, plucked turkey.

"Do you realize, my darling," Robin laughed, "that you have achieved something of a medical record— ten weeks in plaster, and all in the cause of Love. Your poor arm is so wasted away that now I will need to see you twice a week for intensive physiotherapy."

We were hugely delighted with ourselves, although I must say I was appalled at the state of my arm as Robin rubbed some cream into the flaky skin. However, he assured me that once the air got at it, it would start looking human again in a few days.

1943

Warren Farm House (back view), with three of our animal tribe in the foreground: Flack, Pluto, and Towser

Lt. D. (for Donald) M. Judd, D.S.C.

Corporal Muriel
Gane, W. A. A. F.,
1942

Letter informing me
of my commission

12th September 1942

Madam,

I am commanded by the Air Council
to inform you that they have approved your
appointment to a commission in the Women's
Auxiliary Air Force in the rank of Assistant
Section Officer on probation with effect
from 16th September 1942 . You will
remain on probation (normally for a period
of twelve months) until confirmed in your
appointment, which will be for the duration
of hostilities.

Notification accordingly will
appear in the London Gazette.

I am, Madam,
Your obedient Servant,

CA Shearing

A.8764.

Miss. M C. Gane .

W.A.A.F. officers on training course at Bowness, Lake
Windermere, 1943. Section Officer Gane is in the back
row (second from left).

Corporal Gane
after a fencing tournament
at Fighter Command, 1942

Squadron Leader
George Rupert Pushman,
D.F.C., 1943

Our wedding day, with W.A.A.F. Guard of Honour. At St.
Bartholomew's-the-Great, City of London, 1943.

Cardiff Castle

PUCKLECHURCH and I, never compatible, were heading for a separation. Later in January, word came through of an interim posting to Balloon Command, Cardiff. I was overjoyed. It was away from Pucklechurch, but not on the other side of the country from Robin and Bristol.

Just before I was due to leave, a farewell party was organized for me in the Sergeants' Mess. Everyone had clubbed together and bought me a beautiful silver compact, which I kept and cherished for years. The Sergeants' Mess had been the only truly happy place I had known at Pucklechurch, and leaving my friends there was the sole regret I felt in shaking Pucklechurch's dust from my feet.

I was looking forward to Cardiff as I set off on the train. I had felt smothered where I was and hoped the new posting would give me the opportunity to expand my mental horizons. When I set down at the station, I was met by my senior W.A.A.F. officer. She was an older woman, but warm and friendly and seemed delighted to see me. She told me there would be three of us and four R.A.F. officers, and together we would be responsible for eight balloon sites. These were dotted in and around Cardiff, one being in the centre of the docks, the famous Tiger Bay area.

I found our headquarters were in the stables at Cardiff Castle. As we approached, a solitary balloon was flying stoically from the keep. This balloon was to prove a strange sort of spook for me as time went by. I came to watch for it on a crisp winter's night, when I would be coming back up the long drive to the Castle. There would be no sound except the wingeing and creaking of the wire cable. Then my eyes would slowly rise to the lone balloon, shimmering whitely in the wind and casting an eerie shadow above me. I later steeled myself not to look at it, but it was part of the haunting atmosphere of the Castle itself and I would find myself peddling past the old keep as though the Devil were at my heels.

All this, of course, was to come later. Now, as we drove up to the Mess, I was given such a warm welcome that I felt as though I had come into a cozy home, with a fire burning on the hearth and a welcoming drink at the ready. I met the other W.A.A.F. officer and the four men, all of whom put themselves out to be courteous and helpful and let me know how happy they were that I had come to join them.

After a while I was taken over to my quarters, and the next day received a briefing on how things were run. Our main means of transport was via solid, R.A.F. bicycles. The balloon sites were positioned some distance apart, covering the city of Cardiff like a colossal umbrella. The men were responsible for the maintenance of the balloons and winches, and we were in charge of the girl operators. This meant everything that pertained to their well-being and physical health, as well as how they actually operated these vast barrage balloons. Each site had a corporal in charge, and there was a lot of friendly rivalry among the girls on the eight sites. They took tremendous pride in their domains, and it rather reminded me of the little country railway stations before the war, where each station master tried to make his look the most attractive.

My job was to inspect the sites under my control, but I also had to conduct physical training on these sites as well as take classes of R.A.F. servicemen back at the Castle. These latter classes were held at 7:30 a.m., and I had to take a lot of good-natured ribbing from the R.A.F. officers about the sudden enthusiasm they had noticed in their men for turning out on the parade ground. Best of all about my new posting, though, was that my dream of conducting drill was finally being answered. I was assigned the task of working up two flights to a high standard of drill to take part in the Cardiff "Wings for Victory Parade" that was to take place in a few months' time.

With all these varied and absorbing jobs, life passed pleasantly at Cardiff. Happily it was close enough to Bristol that Robin, Peter, Suzy, and I could continue our Saturday night dates at the little club. It was on one of these that Robin and I were sitting between dances when we saw Suzy and Peter coming towards us, their arms entwined around each other, and their faces glowing.

"All right, you two," said Peter, "open the champagne. Suzy, shall we tell them? Of course, we'll tell them," he went on, answering his own question, "we'll tell the whole world. Listen, world, Suzy and I have just got engaged. We're madly, blissfully in love, and we don't intend to wait about. What would you think of coming to a wedding a month today?"

We did not have a chance to say a thing before Peter went on excitedly. "Robin, would you be my best man? And, Moo, Suzy would like your moral support. After all, you were responsible for our meeting in the first place, and we will love you for it forever."

When Peter finally wound down, we were all on our feet, kissing each other and talking at once. To see Suzy so happy was a joy to me, and Peter looked as though he would burst. Please, God, I prayed, don't let anything happen to spoil this for them. Let Peter survive this wretched war, and let them be happy together.

When Robin and I moved back on the dance floor, I knew what was coming. He tried desperately to pin me down. If Peter and Suzy were brave enough to dare fate, why couldn't we? I wanted so much to say yes, and to see the same sort of happiness in his eyes that I had seen in Peter's. Yet always at the back of my mind was Donald, for whom I had promised to wait. Donald, whose letters never mentioned marriage; Donald, who did not believe in commitment in wartime; Donald, whose memory was growing increasingly dim. I could not tell all this to Robin, so I waffled by promising to give him my answer in a few weeks. I pleaded with him to be patient, arguing what were a few weeks more or less if we were to spend our whole life together.

Suzy and I got our heads together over wedding plans. Her elderly parents lived in the North of Scotland, and travel being what it was, that was clearly an impractical venue. The wedding could only take place in London, we reasoned. It was the most central spot for the majority, and Suzy's parents were quite prepared to come down. So, on a lovely day in early spring, Suzy and Peter were married. They both shone with happiness, and I had tears in my eyes when I waved them good-bye.

The War Hits Home

AS I WAS in London on a three-day pass and Robin had to return to Bristol, I decided to go home. I felt I needed time to think, and I needed to see my mother. I adored my father, but it was to my mother that all of us turned if hurt or troubled, or if we had a decision to make. I never ceased to wonder that such indomitability and strength of character could be contained in such a small person. She ran her large household, entertained masses of overseas troops, nursed my sister Audrey, who needed round-the-clock care, and yet she still managed to make each one of us feel special. My homecomings were always treated like gifts from the gods.

It was no different this time. My mother, digging around in her precious store of supplies, had managed to augment my welcome-home dinner into what could pass as a modest wartime feast. Mr. Cuthbert, the man from London, was with us again and had taken his wife to the pictures, then virtuously accompanied her back to the Sisters before returning to the farm. He joined us in the pleasant nightly ritual of a cup of tea before we all took off for our respective beds. Just as I reached the top of the stairs, I heard a powerful, rushing sound, like a frenzied hurricane. I could feel the house sway violently, and for a moment I thought it would be lifted from its foundations by the unbelievable force of this wind. Suddenly there was silence, which was followed almost immediately by a shattering explosion. The poor old house shook and shuddered as though in an epileptic fit. It felt like the end of the world, and I could not begin to guess at what cataclysm was taking place outside.

Fortunately, my father was home that night and began to charge about trying to muster his family into some form of order. He had just been in the act of getting undressed for bed and rushed out into the hall in his underwear. He was a very distinguished looking and dignified man, and seeing him tearing about in his smalls struck me as incredibly funny. The whole household had, by now, gathered in the corridors. My grandmother and her wartime guest, an ancient aunt by adoption, had come out of their quarters at the end of the house, obviously alarmed and a little frightened. Mr. Cuthbert was terrified and made no bones about it. He announced several times to anyone who would listen that he wanted to return to London where at least there were ack-ack guns for the defence of the populace. Flo was flapping around looking for her chicks, and poor Nellie, as deaf as a post, could only wonder what on earth all the commotion was about. Bill, the cowman, and his wife and their two little daughters, aged four and ten months, rushed over from the cottage in a varied assortment of night attire to seek refuge in the big house. The only calm member of the group was my mother, who ordered us to pull ourselves together and get ready to go to the shelter.

She put on an old coat over her nightgown and disappeared out into the dark with our Cowman, followed by my father, pleading with her to come back in. He was still hopping about in his long, knee-length underpants, and the sight reduced my sister Diana and I to uncontrollable laughter.

At this point, the air raid wardens arrived to warn us that a dogfight had taken place over the hospital. In order to escape, the German pilot had off-loaded six bombs, and all of them, they suspected, on our land. The wardens were in a king-size flap, for they were afraid some of them could be time bombs and theoretically could go off willy-nilly at any time. With this news, my father really hit high doh, and demanded that my mother take us all away from the house immediately. We were to go anywhere, he directed rather vaguely, but go we must. With all his agitation, his underpants were now at half-mast, and although what he was saying was eminently sensible, it was almost impossible to take him seriously.

My mother flatly refused to budge. "No, Irving," she said firmly, "if we are to be blown up, we will be blown up. But I intend to stay here at Warren Farm House. Besides," she continued, "to move Audrey at this time of night would be sheer lunacy and probably kill her."

My mother was not much over five feet, but was a force to be reckoned with. The discussion was ended, and we all meekly marched off to the shelter. It was not a proper shelter, but had once been our dairy, and was now solidly reinforced with sandbags. It was about the size of an average garage and was partly below ground, the land sloping up at this end of the farm.

It was cold in there, but my mother had equipped the shelter as best she could with an electric heater, a good collection of chairs, and some basic supplies, including a whole keg of beer. As we all filtered in that night and arranged ourselves around the fire, we looked like a wartime poster for refugee relief. There were my mother and father in their grab-bag attire, and Mr. Cuthbert looking ruffled. There was Audrey on her stretcher bed, and Diana being cuddled by Flo. My grandmother, aged seventy-six, sat together with the maiden aunt, Miss Overton, who had just passed her eightieth birthday. Miss Overton looked exactly like a red Indian squaw. She had wrapped herself in a blanket, and her white hair hung in two plaits on either side of a centre parting. Her heavy eyebrows were jet black, and she stared at us all as though we had just spoken with forked tongues. Nellie managed to look mildly befuddled, as so far no one had really had time to communicate what was going on. Bill's wife, who bore a distinct resemblance to those well-endowed ladies on Blackpool picture postcards, decided to breast-feed her offspring, including the four-year-old. She was totally uninhibited about it, and we had grown quite used to seeing her suddenly open her jumper and produce a vast breast for one or another of her daughters. I think it was a sort of comfort to her. Bill thought so, too, as he always used to say "it soothes 'er" rather as though he were talking about an edgy member of his dairy herd.

As soon as dawn broke, the activity became intense. The army was everywhere and had discovered the other five bombs— two in the garden and three in our fields, all of them time bombs. Those in the garden were, luckily, at the far end and well away from the house. They exploded at twenty-minute intervals and did little damage. The one which had caused all the furore the previous night had exploded in one of the fields. The house and gardens were shrouded in white chalk dust, as though an unseasonal snow had fallen. Word spread throughout the neighbourhood and into Guildford, and it seemed the whole county came to view the enormous crater in the middle of our field. The bomb had been a thousand pounder, and windows had been blown out in quite a number of houses surrounding our land. The strange thing was that none of our animals suffered any ill effects from the blast, even though most of them had been out in the fields. Looking at that massive hole, I wondered if centuries from now people would ask how it came to be there, and speculate on crashing meteors or strange rites practiced by the barbarians of the twentieth century. It is history now, and looking back, I rather wish we had planted a tree nearby with a brass plaque telling the story of that night.

Public Decency

I returned to Cardiff after the high drama of my weekend leave, and had to acknowledge that for the moment, at any rate, this strategic site on the Bristol Channel was a good deal more peaceful than the sleepy little market town of Guildford in the Surrey Downs.

As a matter of fact, life in Cardiff was really very pleasant, particularly after the prickly atmosphere of Pucklechurch. Our quarters were comfortable, and there was a friendly, relaxed feeling in the Mess.

The only problem was that we lived too well, and I began to worry that I would not fit into my uniform if I stayed here for any length of time. The R.A.F. officers, for instance, had a breakfast to which they were addicted— porridge, laden with thick, sweet condensed milk, and topped with treacle. They felt this was too good a routine to keep to themselves, and insisted on ordering it for us. In addition to these sinfully calorific breakfasts, there were some excellent restaurants in nearby Tiger Bay. They had unlimited— well, almost— menus, and no five-shilling restrictions* as in other parts of the country. After a good, healthy gorging at one of these restaurants, I was glad enough to get on my bicycle and pedal a few ounces off on my way back to the Castle.

Tiger Bay was a notorious neighbourhood and out of bounds to all uniformed personnel, so we always went

*The five-shilling restriction in restaurants was part of the Government's rationing programme, and restaurant owners were not allowed to serve food over a five shilling limit.

there in civvies. There was a large black population, as well as a great many foreign sailors, most of them restive after many weeks at sea, and fights seemed to erupt on the slightest pretext. Yet strangely enough, our balloon site, smack in the middle of this explosive area and entirely manned by girls, was never bothered, and no one posted there ever came to any harm during the entire course of the war. At least no harm they did not wish upon themselves.

One day, the corporal in charge of the Tiger Bay site registered a complaint that two of her girls were inviting a couple of West Indian sailors into their Nissen hut at night. Furthermore, they had become so practiced at avoiding detection that whenever anyone went to investigate, the girls were always alone.

Finally a plan was devised worthy of MI5. Two R.A.F. police sergeants and I drove up, leaving our transport some distance from the site so as not to alert the culprits with our headlights. Then the three of us, under the protective cover of dark, crept down the steep, rocky hill to lie in wait for the visitors either to come or go.

After what seemed an interminable time, we heard the creak of a door, and two shadows emerged from the girls' hut. The R.A.F. police swung down on them like Tarzan—minus the yell—and the sounds of a Grade A punch-up ensued. I prayed earnestly that the R.A.F. would be the victors, as I was next in the line of combat and did not feel equal to a couple of rounds with two towering West Indians. Thankfully, the "good guys" triumphed, and the way was clear for me to go into the hut and formally charge the guilty girls with what was a very serious offence. It was a shame, because for a few nights' casual dalliance, they were dishonourably dismissed from the service, and we lost two well-trained balloon operators.

On another occasion, I was alone in the Mess having a quick cup of coffee when the telephone rang. It seemed that a resident in a house in the dock area was telephoning to make a complaint that soldiers in a nearby billet, opposite the W.A.A.F site, were putting "french letters" on the end of a stick and hanging them outside the windows. He was reporting the matter in the interest of public decency and suggested the W.A.A.F. officer in charge deal with the matter at once.

Deal with the matter? The W.A.A.F. officer in charge was puce with embarrassment and desperately trying to think of someone on whom she could fob off this job. The senior W.A.A.F. officer was away on leave, and I simply could not bring myself to discuss so indelicate a matter with the R.A.F. officers. There was no way around it. In the absence of Superman, this was a job for Section Officer Gane.

Unfortunately, Section Officer Gane had never seen a french letter, and for that matter, had never really given a moment's thought to the subject. Probably if I had been shown one, I would have taken it to be a clever little container for keeping money in while swimming.

It was then that I had the brilliant idea of telephoning the army officer in charge of the men's billet. As a disembodied voice on the telephone, my blushes would remain unseen and unsuspected. So quickly before anyone returned, I dialled the number, heart pounding, and asked to speak to the duty officer. When he eventually came on the line, I was ready for him. Taking a colossal breath, I lashed into the poor fellow like an outraged madame, ranting on about "my girls," the obscenity of the whole thing, and slipshod discipline, until I finally ran out of breath. I had obviously left the poor, unfortunate officer totally nonplussed and without a shred of defence. He burst into profuse apologies and assured me that such a thing would never, ever happen again. He was still making abject squeaks as I put down the receiver.

Some weeks later, I happened to meet an officer at some Air Force function, and found out by chance that it was he to whom I had been speaking that night. What a shock! He was if anything younger than I, downy-cheeked and looking as though his Nanny were not far behind him. I recoiled inwardly at all the things I had said to him, as looking at him now, I realized his blushes must have matched my own. Needless to say, I never let on who had been on the other end of the telephone, and nobody in our Mess ever heard of the incident, which happily for all concerned was never repeated.

For the most part, I concentrated on training my two flights in drilling for the big Victory Parade. All the girls were as keen as I, and I have to admit, in all modesty, that the end result was close to perfection. The day of the parade was clear and bright, and as both my father and Robin had arranged to come down for the event, I managed to bring them together before the parade actually started. They liked each other immediately, as I had been sure they would, so I fell into line at the head of my girls with a light heart, and a lighter step.

The Mayor and Mayoress of Cardiff headed the parade, followed by city dignitaries, the three Services, the Voluntary Service, the Scouts and the Guides, and a superb turnout of brass bands. Our flights were following the R.A.F. detachment, and with the sound of the R.A.F. march in our ears, every spine stiffened, every shoulder squared, and every head lifted. There was a gratifying response from the crowd lining the pavement, and the money raised was beyond all expectations.

Death Duties

DESPITE the pleasant life at Cardiff, I was still going through a certain amount of emotional turmoil and realized I would have to come to a decision about Robin very soon. Suzy and Peter were living near Barrow Gurney in a charming, honey-coloured cottage, with a thatched roof and roses blooming around the door. It was idyllic and so were they— deeply in love and blissfully happy. Whenever Robin and I visited them, we both left feeling how much we, too, wanted this sort of happiness. I realized now that I wanted to marry Robin as much as he wanted to marry me. The only thing holding me back was the knowledge that I would have to write to Donald and tell him. Even if the letter did not reach him for months, I felt that I could not honourably say yes to Robin until I had sent the Message to Donald on its way.

I dreaded having to do it, but put the blame squarely where it belonged— on the bloody, awful war. Had it not been for the war, I thought, I would have been married to Donald by now and be on my way to living happily ever after. Instead, here I was about to destroy the promise of trust we had made to each other. Still, I had now made another promise, which was to give Robin my decision at the end of the week, and I felt happier now that I knew what it would be.

In the meantime, rumours were flying about Cardiff that an ammunition ship was being loaded in the docks. Stories spread that German Intelligence had been tipped off, and planned an attack on Cardiff docks during the early hours of Friday morning. All Cardiff was in a state of apprehension, holding its breath against the horrendous possibility of half the city being obliterated if the Germans should get a direct hit. What nobody knew was that, thanks to British Intelligence, the ammunition ship had already slipped silently out of the harbour the previous night.

The Germans came just the same. In the early hours of the next morning, we were awakened by the heart-stopping wail of the air raid sirens. Immediately we scrambled out of bed, grabbed our clothes, ran to our bicycles, and raced down the long Castle drive to spread out like a fan, each of us going to a different balloon site. The R.A.F. officers covered the site in the docks, in order that they could get to any one of the other seven sites quickly if a calamity occurred.

As I pedalled frantically, I had to admit to myself that I was terrified. The noise of the guns blazing away in the dark was deafening, and I felt, rather irrationally, that I was alone in a city on the brink of destruction. With the exception of the odd policeman or air raid warden, I saw no one about, until my bicycle was joined on the main road by fire engines and ambulances, coming and going in all directions. Dear God, I prayed, please don't let me be killed tonight. A line from some half-forgotten poem filtered into my mind—"nor let me die before I have begun to live." I think I was crying, but being so alone, consoled myself with the knowledge that no one would ever know.

I arrived at the balloon site. All was calm. While the world exploded around them, these incredible girls were quietly tending their balloons. I sent a silent thank-you towards the heavens for our safety to this point, followed by another flurry of prayers to keep it that way.

"Hello, ma'am," said the Corporal as I dismounted, "would you like a cup of tea?"

Tea—good God, I thought. "Why yes," I answered as calmly as though I were at a vicar's garden party. "Shall we all have one?"

I think underneath we all felt an almost unbearable tension, but each of us was determined to conceal it from the others. The girls seemed to be glad I was there, although not for any good I did. It was just being there, I suppose. The violence of the raid increased, and finally we had to dash into the little air raid shelter on the site and sit it out in the dark. The only comfort was the proximity of others. We were packed in and felt the closeness, emotionally as well as physically. None of us spoke, listening instead to the terrible, persistent bombing in the world outside our temporary cocoon of safety.

It was not until daybreak that the full horror became known. One of our balloon sites up on a hill on the far side of the city had received a direct hit, blowing the Nissen hut to smithereens and instantly killing several of the girls. The pretty little corporal in charge had her arm and shoulder blown off and suffered dreadful damage to one side of her face. In this appalling condition, she had managed to crawl to the Pioneer Corps position— nearly a quarter of a mile away— to raise the alarm. She had only been married the previous week, and her husband, an able seaman in the Navy, had just left for sea duty, destination unknown.

The ruin of these young lives, and the feeling of sick helplessness at the carnage of that night, marked a watershed in my life. Painful as my wartime losses had been, I had not been there at the ending of lives dear to me. I had been able to protect myself by giving dignity and purpose to their deaths, mentally burying the realities in flag-draped coffins. Now, as I stood with the other officers while parts of bodies were collected, I found myself shivering despite the warm sunshine. No one spoke and no one cried. The hurt was too deep, and our eyes too dry for tears. How could all this youth and freshness, this joy and promise, have ended in these torn, sad remnants?

Some of the R.A.F. officers had served in the First World War. They had seen such sights before, and their instinct was to protect us, but they also knew that dealing with these situations was part of being an officer. It was something we had to face. We had been instructed at O.C.T.U. as to what to do in case of death in the ranks. I knew the drill but had never imagined having to do it. Now the unthinkable had happened, and there was nothing for it but to do my job along with everyone else.

The first thing was to try to restore some sort of order on the site. Once the bodies had been taken away, we began to sort through everything that was recognizable. The girls' private possessions were scattered and strewn everywhere, like the contents of some intimate drawer plundered by vandals. In some strange way, I think we all felt we owed it to the dead to save these echoes of their lives from impersonal curiosity. We carefully gathered up everything, no matter how trivial, and listed each item before packing them into boxes.

My senior officer had the terrible task of informing the families. The poor little corporal was on the danger list. Her husband had been contacted at sea and was being brought home. The day was the longest I had ever known. We worked tirelessly until all the ends of this awful tragedy had been neatly tied.

The next week was a blur. Nothing seemed quite real. We were called upon to accompany the bodies to their respective home towns and attend the funerals alongside the families. I was emotionally keyed up with pity, concern, and nerves, but what does remain in my mind after all these years was the pride and unaffected dignity with which these ordinary and unheroic people buried their children. It is considered hopelessly square today to extol the old British virtues— staunchness in adversity, love of country, valour in battle. Yet they were virtues; they did exist, and we believed in them. There were no parents to whom I spoke during that agonizing week who did not truly believe that the daughters they loved had died with honour in a just cause.

I had never been to a funeral before, and having to attend so many was physically and emotionally draining. I suddenly realized that I had been so caught up in the tragic sequence of events that I had not once thought of Robin or of family. None of them knew what had happened. I would have to get in touch as soon as possible, I thought, but I still had one more duty to perform. I must visit Betsy, the corporal who had sounded the alarm. When I went into her room, her new husband was sitting beside her holding her hand. They looked so young and vulnerable that my throat ached with pity. Betsy mustered a pale smile for me and bravely asked for details, which I tried to skim over for her sake.

By the time I returned to the Castle, I felt flattened by fatigue. The R.A.F. officers gave me a warm and comforting welcome, and poured me a very stiff whiskey. It is a drink I still loathe, but it was certainly the right medication for the moment. I downed it and thought wearily that when the other W.A.A.F. officers returned from the funerals in Scotland, perhaps at last we could get back to some degree of normalcy.

As I turned to go up to bed, I looked at the notice board and saw that I had had several calls from Commander Robin Hayes and two from my father. I was too tired to think of anything but a soak in a tub, and of falling into bed. They will ring again, I thought, as I went into my room. My eyes fell on a stack of letters on my dresser. I saw my father's distinctive handwriting on one; another from my grandmother, and another from dear Liz. The one I wanted most of all—a letter from Robin—was there at the bottom of the pile.

I sank back on my bed, clutching my letters, and opened the one from Robin. It began: "Darling, where have you been? I have been desperately trying to make contact. I am beside myself with worry, as I could get no sense out of the people answering the telephone. They just kept saying you were away on duty. The fact is, I have been posted to a hospital somewhere in the Far East, leaving on Thursday. The thought of going without seeing you is driving me crazy. We have so much to finalize— our wedding for one thing. I have been dreaming of the moment when you will look at me with those incredible eyes of yours and tell me at last you will marry me. As soon as you get back, please, please telephone and put me out of my misery."

I could not read any further; tears were falling on the paper and blurring the ink. Thursday, Robin had said, and here it was Saturday. I turned and buried my head in the pillows. I had not only missed saying good-bye to this most wonderful of men, but above all, I had missed telling him what he most wanted to hear, that yes . . . *yes* . . . *YES* . . . I would marry him. It was more than I could bear. The Far East was a world away, and as with Donald, it could be years before we met again. The thought brought fresh floods of tears. The person I loved more than anything else in the world was gone, without a good-bye and without his longed-for promise. I could only pray that he would believe in me until I could write to him.

On this poignant thought, I fell asleep, exhausted by the expenditure of so much emotion on top of the tragedy and horror of the week that had just passed.

Glorious Surroundings

DOORS CLOSE and doors open. I went down to breakfast the next morning, leaden of heart, and picked up a letter addressed to me from the Air Ministry. What next, I thought, as I slit it open. I read it, at first with disbelief, then with growing excitement, and finally with elation. I, Section Officer Gane, had been selected to attend a Senior W.A.A.F. Officer's Course at Bowness, Lake Windermere, in the Lake District. What was that line about "when our need was the sorest"? I began to have new faith in a kindly Providence.

I had only been given a week's notice, which was just as well as I had little time to dwell on the past horrendous week, nor on the sadness of saying farewell to the kind, good friends I had made in the Mess at Cardiff.

The course at the Lakes was to last a month, and I was looking forward to it. It was not just the challenge of the course itself, but I had never been to that part of the country and had heard all my life how beautiful it was. When I told my family, my father was delighted. He was now in charge of factory security in MI5, and in the course of his duties he was called upon to make periodic inspections at Seascale, on the coast of Cumberland. He promised to visit me en route, and if possible take me along with him on one of his trips. I sensed he and my mother were worried about me, feeling that the succession of calamities in my life was beginning to tell. I knew this was true, and was pleased to be going to a place whose beauty, I was convinced, would provide a restorative to my bruised spirit.

My father travelled to Windermere with me before continuing on to Seascale. On the train we talked of happy things, and by the time I reached my destination, I found myself beginning to relax. I wondered if any of my O.C.T.U. friends would be on the course, or anyone I knew for that matter.

I had just descended from the ancient taxi that had wheezed its way up to the gate of my new billet, a posh resort hotel called the Bellsfield, when I heard someone shout, "Muriel, hello. It's great to see you. Look everybody, it's Muriel!"

I turned and was thrilled to see several of my old friends from O.C.T.U. We all started talking at once, asking questions, recalling people, and gossiping about who was where. We sounded like a flock of starlings on the rise. "Wait until you see who else is here," somebody said to me. I glanced around, and standing on the portico looking as though she could not contain herself for another second, was my dearest friend Liz. We rushed toward each other and went through what was almost a parody of a reunion scene. We would bestow a hug, then stand at arm's length surveying one another unbelievingly, then indulge in another spontaneous hug.

"Liz," I said, "this is absolutely marvellous. In my wildest dreams I never dared imagine that I would be so lucky as to see you here at Windermere."

"Neither did I, Moo. We have so much to catch up on. Can you believe it's almost a year since we last met? I've managed to bag us a super room overlooking the lake. It's a suite, actually, with a small sitting room and the most sumptuous bathroom ever. The furniture is no great shakes, but with a little joint imagination, it will be a palace."

We continued to talk all through my unpacking and through supper, after which we slipped off to a nearby pub. By the time we returned to our quarters, the secrets of the last few months had been thoroughly aired and discussed.

The course proved demanding but rewarding, and to be able to train in such glorious surroundings was a bonus in itself. We found to our delight that we could hire bicycles and rowboats. It was heaven, at the end of a busy week, to take a picnic, organize a boat, and row over to Ambleside. We had been told that this site in the Lake District had been chosen mainly for its remoteness and lack of outside distractions. It was a W.A.A.F. stronghold, with only the trainees and the course instructors in residence. Yet word spread as word will. Shortly after the training centre was established, it was amazing how many lonely air crews seemed to develop a sudden interest in the Lakes as a place to spend their weekends.

There were Australians stationed at two points relatively nearby and again it was remarkable how often girls would cycle over the hills from Bowness, and Aussies would pedal their way across the fells from Penrith or Carlisle, only to meet up "by chance" at one of the charming lake-side country pubs. I remember one pub in particular that had the gorgeous name of "The Drunken Duck," a title acquired, I was told, from the habit the locals had of standing the denizens of the duck pond a pint or two on a Saturday night.

If the weekends were escape into a forgotten holiday world, the weeks were rigorous training. I was surprised at the breadth of the course and the range of the tests we were given. One such was having to make a three-minute speech, with no prior warning as to what the subject might be. I remember having "cotton wool" thrown at me, and being amazed at how fluent one could be on so dull a topic.

The end of the course came too quickly, with both Liz and I once again congratulating each other as we passed with superior grades. It was what I needed to regain my confidence and perspective. It had been good for me, too, to have Liz working beside me again. It was a relief to be able to give voice to my worries, and somehow they did not seem so dark and unbearable when shared. Liz, herself, was incredibly happy. She had become engaged to an

American flyer, and they planned to marry in July. She wanted me to be her bridesmaid, to which I gladly agreed. I met David when Liz and I travelled to Paddington together, and his eyes lit up every time he looked at her. Yes, Liz is lucky, I thought.

Spring Back

I HAD TWO whole glorious weeks' leave before reporting to my new post, R.A.F. Flying Training Command, Brize Norton in Oxfordshire. I was feeling better about life, but I still needed to unwind after a month of intensive training, and home shimmered in my mind like a mirage in the desert.

Our house had shed some of its evacuees, and the guests were now of an entirely different nature. For one thing, my mother, being a Canadian, had opened our home to Canadian servicemen, and it seemed to me countless numbers filed through Warren Farm House during the war years. Some dropped by in passing, so to speak, for a "cuppa" and a chat, while others came regularly when on leave. My mother's open-handed hospitality required no prior notice of arrival. She adored having her countrymen come in their dozens, and they, in their turn, felt a link with home in my mother's Canadian accent and store of overseas parcels. At Christmas, my father was sent out to tour the streets of Guildford, gathering up servicemen like abandoned fledglings, and bringing them back to the farm for a family Christmas dinner.

Even within the family, things had changed dramatically. My sister Audrey had made an almost miraculous recovery under circumstances which are a story in themselves. Although still only seventeen, she had managed to get into the Motor Transport Corps and was away as often as she was home. Diana was now in boarding school in Dorset; Flo had been called up now that she had no children to look after, and was presently serving as a charge hand in the N.A.A.F.I. in Aldershot. Bill, our Cowman, had left as well, and was on duty for the Agricultural Committee, delivering potatoes to the army barracks at Aldershot. Tony Howarth, our medical student, had gone, as had the evacuee children, and the farm seemed strangely hushed and abandoned as I came up our long drive to the house.

It was a beautiful morning. I swear nowhere in the world can spring be lovelier than in England. The orchards were seas of pink and white blossoms, the lilac was ready to flower, and in the deep green of the moss at the edge of the woods were myriads of violets and anemones. The old chestnut tree stood guard in the courtyard as it always had, with Pluto's kennel like a small guardhouse alongside it. My mother was standing at the door as though sensing my arrival, and as I rounded the corner I ran into her arms.

Together we went into the kitchen for a cup of tea from the old brown teapot that never seemed to be allowed to cool down. The cupboard door was ajar and I caught sight of an enchanting new litter of kittens. We always had kittens in the kitchen— once as many as seventeen— and all in an interesting range of colours as the adverts say. Nellie had some baby budgies in the nesting box in her bird cage, and both progeny and proud parents were creating the most almighty racket. Nellie, deaf as she was, was mercifully unaware of the row. I almost tripped over the dogs who clustered their welcome around my feet. There was no question about it: changes or not, I was home.

There was one enormous gap in the close world of Warren Farm House that I tried not to think about, steering my mind away from the painful reality. On every other leave, one of my first actions on coming through the door was to dash upstairs to see my grandmother. I found it unbearable to think that I would never see her again, as she had died suddenly of influenza when I was on my course. We had been friends, my grandmother and I, and one of my delights had been to cozy up beside the fire in her little flat and tell her both my triumphs and disasters, always sure of a sympathetic and remarkably sage ear. She was a perfectionist, and those things she taught me to do, like needlework, I still do to this day as though her patient but demanding spirit were looking over my shoulder.

At least, I thought, even though the farm might not be quite as exciting as it had been, it is good to see my mother a little less pressured. Not one to sit with her hands folded, however, she had turned her considerable energies into the art of animal husbandry. She had begun to rear pigs and had doubled her complement of turkeys and chickens. She read everything she could on the subject and had become quite engrossed in chopping up nettles and hard-boiled eggs for her turkey chicks. She always had a witches' cauldron of chicken swill boiling away on the gas ring. It looked loathsome, a revolting mush of potato peelings and any other sort of food scrap that came to hand. The chickens revelled in it, however, and paid her back handsomely by laying the most wonderful dark brown eggs. Her turkeys were orphaned and were reared by a redoubtable little bantam hen called "Banty." She was a tiny, self-important miniature, but took great delight in bossing her foster children, all of whom towered over her as she led them proudly around the courtyard. Banty came to her end through the stratagems of a wily old fox, and the entire family went into mourning.

My leave unfolded like a flower in the warmth of that glorious spring. Day followed day, and although I missed having Diana to ride with me, I was blissfully content just to take Sally into every loved and remembered corner of the countryside. With a picnic lunch and the dogs in tow, I would start along Pilgrim's Way to the bluebell woods, picking my way carefully over the flowering carpet, through the bright new shoots of bracken, and finally up the sandy hillock to St. Martha's Church. As a child, it had seemed to me that while God had perhaps been unkind to set St. Martha's on such a lonely hillside, He had compensated by giving her the magnificent guard of fir trees that encircled her like a protective castle wall.

There is a special feeling about churches when no one else is there, and I hitched Sally up to the wicket gate and made my way inside. I prayed as only the young can pray that God would keep Robin safe and "make everything all right." The minutes ticked by in the silent church, and finally I rose to my feet, walked through the old, creaking door and into the brilliance of the spring sunshine.

I continued across the fields to the Silent Pool at Shere, and by way of Newlands Corner on our homeward journey. Sally's great thrill was to come home by way of the seventeenth hole of the golf course, for she knew she was nearly home. At this landmark it was her wits against mine, for she danced and pranced and spun around, trying every trick she knew to get the bit between her teeth for a final full gallop home. I, on the other hand, had to let her know she had a rider and could not always have her own way. It was a very steep switch back, and I would invariably assert my will while going down the hill and then would suddenly surprise her by giving her her head. She would be off like Pegasus, mane and tail flowing in the wind. By the time we reached the end of Merrow Downs, I would turn around and see the tribe of dogs stumbling over themselves to catch up with us in order that we could all make it home together.

I had just come in from one such lovely day when my mother came out to greet me with some letters in her hand. We sauntered out into the garden where Nellie had set out a delicious tea, eked out on ration books, overseas parcels, and gifts from the visiting Canadians. It had been such a gorgeous day, and I was happy to sink down on the lawn with my clutch of letters. I saw that I had received one from Suzy. Dear Suzy, I thought, I have not seen her since Cardiff. I wonder how she is getting on. I unfolded the sheets and began to read, and as I read I felt my whole body begin to stiffen. I saw the print in front of me, but its message did not seem to be penetrating my mind. I wanted to say something to my mother, but I seemed to have no voice and could not move a muscle.

"Whatever is wrong, darling?" my mother asked. When I did not reply, she came protectively to my side, and taking the letter from me, read for herself the news that had turned me to stone. Suzy had been asked by Peter to write to tell me that Robin's ship had been torpedoed, and there had been no survivors. They were heartbroken, but realized that their heartbreak was nothing compared to what I must be feeling . . . could I not come and stay? Was there anything they could do? The letter went on, full of kind, futile phrases that I could not absorb. I *knew*, I thought, I always *knew*. Loss was the dark side of love. This was the shadowy, unidentifiable fear that had been with me ever since I got Robin's letter in Cardiff. It had stayed with me through the weeks of my training and had not left me, even in the sunlit hours of my leave. Robin and I had been too much in love, perhaps, and had earned the envy of the gods. It had, literally, been too good to be true. As the numbness left me, my mind whirled through agonies of regret . . . if only I had telephoned him during that fateful week in Cardiff . . . if only I had given him my answer and sent him off with a promise . . . if only . . . if only.

I turned at last to my mother. "Oh, Mummy, I can't seem to cry anymore. Where have all my tears gone. I just ache. I don't feel there is anything left anymore . . . my life is shattered. Oh, why didn't I marry him— I would have had something of him forever— not this terrible, empty wasteland I am in now . . ." I broke off as the benison of tears finally came, and I found myself sobbing in my mother's arms.

My mother kept her thoughts to herself as I clung to her. She knew that nothing she could say now would comfort me, and it was not until years later that she told me what she had been thinking on that desolate afternoon. Here is a girl, she thought, with the mind and emotions of a mature woman, who must now sort out her life for herself. God knows, I experienced the same heartbreaks in the

First World War and truly believed I would never get over them. But I did, and so will this poor child, my daughter. Pray God, I will always be there when she needs me, but let it be as equals. Let her find her way and the strength to know that life is not over.

Had I known my mother's thoughts at that moment, I would not have believed the truth in them. I was convinced that this was a blow from which I would never recover. All the bright hope of my new posting at Brize Norton was now simply something to be lived through if possible. My father came home that evening and was alarmed at my obvious distress. He was too kind to probe, but suggested that the two of us go for a walk after dinner.

As we strolled down the flowering lane that had seemed so beautiful only a few hours before, he told me that he could offer no real comfort to me at the moment but that perhaps he might be able to help me get my thoughts into perspective again.

"What is heartbreak now, my dear," he said "will, I promise you, be a thing of the past in six months' time. We are given, some of us, great problems in life, and it is the way that we solve them, and overcome them, that builds our character. Our lives, like a book, are made up of a series of chapters, some happy, some funny, some colourless, and some desperately sad. We have to live through our book until the end, and it is only then that the book can be judged on its merit, or lack of merit. We have been so proud of the way you have tackled this period in your life, and equally proud of the way you have handled the blows you have suffered. I know children do not like their parents to talk of God, but I most profoundly believe He is there, and that from Him comes our strength in dark times. Now, my dear, I know you can not accept everything I have said right now, but in six months from now I will remind you of this talk we have had together."

After a few lost days spent in the limbo of grief, I began to surface once more. Human beings, particularly young human beings, are resilient creatures, and I slowly gathered myself together and decided rather forlornly that life would not wait for me forever. I looked in the mirror and felt the first faint flutterings of a returning self-image. I looked a mess. My face was puffy and my eyes were blurred and red-rimmed. My hair was lank, dull, and faintly sticky looking. I went into the bathroom and washed my face. Then I made an appointment at the hairdresser. It was the first step on the road back.

A Happy Posting

BRIZE NORTON lay ahead, and by the end of my leave I had begun to welcome it. It was a new experience and perhaps if I threw myself into work, I might be able to forget for a little while that Robin was gone, and bit by bit the pain might gradually lessen.

My father was returning to Woodstock, so we planned to travel together. We arrived at the R.A.F. station and I reported to the Guardroom, where they directed me to the Officers' Mess. Brize Norton had been an established Air Force base in the pre-war years, and everything was laid out in a prescribed pattern. The Mess was close to the Station Commander's house, which was in a position of supremacy, followed by the married quarters of other officers, all arranged in the correct pecking order. As we drove towards the Mess, I noticed the Airborne Division was also on the station, and the thought of dashing Army parachutists caused a slight stir of interest. I must be feeling better, I thought.

I said good-bye to my father, then turned and mounted the steps towards the entrance to the Mess. A W.A.A.F. squadron officer was awaiting my arrival. I saluted, and she returned it with a smile. She was a natural, relaxed sort of person, and we fell easily into conversation. Over a cup of tea she apologized for the cramped conditions in the W.A.A.F. officers' house. She hoped they would be able to make changes for the better within the next few days. The other officers filtered in for tea. Introductions were made, and I felt intuitively that this would be a happy posting. I was asked to be over at the Mess around seven o'clock for drinks and introductions all around. I recalled, with a shiver, the coldness of my welcome at Pucklechurch and could not help but be aware of the difference. The W.A.A.F. house was, as stated, a bit overcrowded, but it was friendly and companionable, and it did not take long before I began to feel relatively at home.

There was, however, still the ordeal of my first entry into the Mess. By now I had made a number of similar entrances, but I still felt like a slave girl about to go on the auction block. For one thing, an Air Force Mess is primarily a male domain, and I was never quite able to rid myself of a feeling of intrusion.

The New Girl Entrance followed a prescribed pattern. First, there was the gradual fading away of conversation as she came in; then there was the slow pivoting of heads in the direction of the door. At this point she would walk into the room, blushing furiously if she were anything like me, and find something fascinating about her feet. Finally when she would sell her soul for a cloak of invisibility, someone would offer a drink. She would take it like a life preserver, and suddenly everybody would start talking again. She was in.

Having gone through all these phases and survived the trial of inspection, I started to look around me. I saw that Brize Norton was, by and large, a young Mess, with a cross-section of R.A.F. and Airborne (the Army's air division). After a little while, I became aware that I was the centre of some sort of joke, which involved wagers being taken on "would he, or wouldn't he, and how long would it take?"

It turned out that the Station Commander, divorced and presumably on the prowl, had a very large house. Knowing the crowded conditions at the W.A.A.F. house, he had a legitimate excuse for offering accommodation to some of the girls on the base. He was selective in his hospitality, however, and only proffered invitations to those who were young, attractive, and unattached. It did not take long before my possibilities were assessed, and a book on the C.O.'s intentions was opened.

Next morning, I had a better chance to see what Brize Norton was all about. As a matter of fact, it was the first R.A.F. station to which I had been posted. Bentley Priory was Fighter Command Headquarters, and as such was more like a small town, incorporating senior officers, civilians, the R.A.F., and the Army, in the presence of a famous Guards regiment. Then there was R.A.F. Pucklechurch (shudder), a Balloon Command base, as was Cardiff. Admittedly I had happy, as well as sad, memories of the Castle, but it was a "place" rather than an active wartime station, and I knew I was missing out on a lot by what Liz and others posted to stations had reported to me.

I was musing away on what my future would be at Brize Norton when I heard a knock at the door. A pretty girl popped her head around in answer to my "come in."

"Hello," she said, "it's Muriel, isn't it? I've come to collect you. I thought it might help if I took you over to the Administration Block and showed you your office. It's all so strange on the first morning, isn't it? Never mind, you'll soon get to know your way around, and if you want some help, just call on me."

I thanked her warmly, grateful for her thoughtfulness and consideration. Her name was Ruth, and as the weeks passed we became very good friends. We set off on a tour of the station, and I was aware that it had a settled and established feeling that had been lacking in most of the bases I had been on before. The paths, between neatly-mown grass, were lined with trees, and there were formal rose beds everywhere. As we rounded the bend in the path, I saw a senior officer coming towards us with a small entourage in tow.

"Here comes the C.O.," Ruth muttered out of the side of her mouth, as we both gave him a snappy salute.

"W-e-1-1," Ruth speculated as we continued on, "haven't you been given the once-over!"

"Rubbish," I replied, "I doubt if he even saw me, we passed by so quickly."

Ruth just laughed, and as we entered the office she announced to the group who were there: "Well, everyone, the great man has cast his eyes on the newcomer, and I am cutting the odds from three days down to two. Any bets?" I found myself blushing furiously, as everyone began laughing and laying— or pretending to lay— wagers.

Once I got down to work in the office that first morning, I found out that I had been brought to Brize Norton to do a very specific job. It seemed that there was a great shortage of flight mechanics, and as a result, girls were being taken from Balloon Command to be re-trained as mechanics. It was not a popular move for the balloon operators. Not only had most of them loved their work with balloons, but as members of small, self-contained units, they had known an unusual degree of independence as well. In addition, they had had the advantage of working in the open air, and apart from the congestion found on most bases. Now, here they were, where they did not want to be, where they had not asked to come, where they had to learn a trade they knew nothing about and were not keen to learn. My job was to work with them as their personal officer. The Powers-That-Be had selected me, feeling that having been in Balloon Command myself, I might have an understanding of their problems and be able to help them overcome their hostility to this new assignment.

Well, I thought, when I heard what was required of me, they may be disappointed, but this is exactly what I have been waiting for. I was to be in charge of fifty girls, and my mind had already whirred ahead to some hazy future point at which "my girls," impeccably drilled, were the acknowledged pride of the W.A.A.F. and the envy of all. I lost some of the fire of this vision when later on that afternoon I assembled a sullen and uninterested group for the purpose of an introductory talk. They were as unhappy a gathering as it is possible to imagine. This is not going to be easy, I thought, as I prepared to mount the platform. No, I thought again, psychologically the platform puts me in the position of talking down to them. I want them to feel that I am one of them, also torn away from Balloon Command. At that juncture, I spotted an old chair, and pulling it up close to the front row, I stood up on it and began to speak.

"Hello, everybody! My name is Muriel Gane. I have just come here from Balloon Command, Cardiff, and I suspect you can imagine how I am feeling. Anyone who has served in the Balloon Command knows how special it is, and I am missing it just as much as you are. (Liar, I thought inwardly, as I continued on.) Still, I have been sent here to be your own personal officer, and I know I am lucky to have you, and I hope you will feel the same way about me, *because,*" I went on, pausing for dramatic effect, "I can assure you that within a month—no, I'll correct that—within two weeks, we are going to be the smartest flight the Air Force has ever seen—anywhere! Everyone will be talking about the special W.A.A.F. flight at Brize Norton, and that special flight will be you—and me," I added with what I hoped was disarming modesty. "Together we will set such a high standard that we will be representing the W.A.A.F. at every Wings for Victory Parade anybody ever heard of. I am not going to pretend it won't be a lot of hard work, because it will, but I hope we can get there together."

I climbed down, flushed and a bit overcome by my own eloquence. The response was electric. They were all around me, asking questions and swearing that I was right. If they were good enough for Balloon Command, they had to be the best at anything else. It was all they had needed, and in a glow of genuine pleasure that I had pulled it off, I made my way back to the quarters.

Opening the door of my bedroom, I noticed two envelopes on my chest of drawers. I opened the top one which was unstamped, and found it was from the Station Commander. It read: "Dear Section Officer Gane—I understand the W.A.A.F. officers' quarters are rather cramped. There are two spare rooms in my house, and I would be delighted to offer these to you and any friend you might wish to invite. I shall look forward with pleasure to seeing you for cocktails at 6 p.m."

He had signed off conventionally as being sincerely mine, and I suddenly started to laugh. I had out-foxed the bookies in the Mess. There they had been, laying odds that I would be installed within two days or three days, and I had made it to the winning gate in less than twenty-four hours. I did not have the slightest hesitation in accepting. It was cramped in our present quarters, and I would be well chaperoned. I packed my bags and waited for Ruth to return. I would ask her to come with me to take up residence in our new, and no doubt much more luxurious, abode.

At six o'clock I presented myself at the C.O.'s house and was welcomed into a gracious drawing room by the host himself. He was blond, very handsome and oozed charm. You would have to have been blind not to see that he was a womanizer, but after almost three years in the Air Force this held no fears for me. Besides, he had the good taste to have photographs of his children well displayed as well as a Lenare studio portrait of a very beautiful woman, whom I took to be his lady of the moment.

The room had lovely high windows and looked out on the runways, which was really quite exciting, as aircraft were taking off and landing almost constantly. The C.O. paid me a head-turning degree of attention, and it would have been impossible not to have been flattered by his charm.

After cocktails, Ruth and I selected our rooms, unpacked our things, and went forth to the Mess for dinner. Needless to say, the news had spread like wildfire that I had beaten the odds, and as we entered the room, I was greeted by a lot of good-natured ribaldry and teasing.

It was a beautiful, early summer evening, and after dinner it was suggested that we all cycle over to the Swan at Minster Lovell, about three miles away. I found myself cycling beside a captain in the Airborne Division called Rory. He looked just like Errol Flynn, with the same engaging lop-sided smile, and in the weeks that followed we saw a lot of each other. He was an athlete, and we found we enjoyed many sports in common. We used to dash off to the tennis courts after a gruelling day and would play late into the evening, until the summer sun finally set and the light faded.

We were both attracted to each other, but with barriers of reserve: he, because like Donald he did not believe in strong wartime attachments, and me, because I did not feel ready to cope with any deep emotional relationship. Sadly, we were both right. Rory was killed at the Battle of Arnhem, as were a number of other friends from Airborne who were with us at Brize Norton.

All these years later, I realize that these companions are not forgotten in my mind. I hear or see something that conjures up a memory, not only of place and time, but of the individuals whose lives touched mine. Not long ago, I was watching a television programme about what happened to the English girls who married American servicemen. For a moment, I was back to the kitchen in the C.O.'s house, sharing a cup of late night cocoa with a pretty little W.A.A.F. called Megan, who used to do the cooking there. She married an American and went to live in the United States. In memory, she is young, rose-complexioned, and very British. In reality, she is probably a very American grandmother with a mid-Atlantic accent and a passion for hot dogs.

What Goes Up . . .

M AY WAS now at its height. The weather was marvellous, and it was pure delight to cycle along the flowering lanes to one of the many charming little pubs in the Oxfordshire countryside. My residency at the Station Commander's was, over all, a satisfactory arrangement, although occasionally he would assume a rather proprietary air and let me know that he was not keen on my going out every evening. I suspected he was lonely, being as he was a man apart. Although he seemed old to us, he was not that old, and being the Station Commander, he could not seem to be favouring one officer over another. I would occasionally meet him in London for dinner and dancing, and I think we both enjoyed those evenings. He understood how I felt, and while he probably cherished some hopes, he was never demanding nor did he ever put me in a position where it would have been impossible for me to meet him again in this way.

My main pleasure at Brize Norton, however, was actually the serious business of training my W.A.A.F.'s. At the end of the predicted fortnight, they were already showing the promise of a highly-trained drilling flight. It was a joy to my heart to see the admiration they received as they marched past. Their whole outlook had changed, and the training instructors were delighted with their progress. It was decided, as a measure of continuing encouragement, that at the end of each week, the most promising trainees would be allowed to fly in a Whitley bomber, or a Horsa glider, as a reward for effort.

Personally, I was not all that sure it was that much of a reward, but the girls seemed thrilled. By way of explanation, I should add that essentially Brize Norton was a flying training station. These Whitley bombers were crewed by bomber pilots on rest from bombing operations. The bombers would take off, towing a huge Horsa, which was flown by an Airborne pilot. At some stage in the course of the flight, the tow rope would be cast off, leaving the glider to its own devices. It looked like some huge bird, soaring and swooping, searching for wind currents to keep it aloft.

In any event, with this bright idea of a free ride as a reward, it looked as though, after all this time in the Air Force, I would at last get the chance to go up in the air. If I could have had any say in the matter, I doubt I would have chosen a Horsa glider to make my flying debut. As it was, I was given no option but was told firmly that it was my job to accompany these girls on their flights. I did not enjoy the experience. It was Oxford and all her many spires that put me off to begin with. Passing over a skyline that resembles a metal pinholder used by flower arrangers, in a hulking glider with a trainee pilot at the controls, was not my idea of a really good time. The roaring of the wind as we scraped over the city was deafening, and the glider, big as it was, seemed suddenly terribly frail—a thing made of match boxes and perishable canvas. I had not really given much thought to "what goes up must come down" and I reached panic point when the horrible thing aimed its Durante nose and dived, hell for leather, toward the earth. This is it, I thought, clutching the seat in a death grip. Then, quite suddenly, the pilot pulled back the control column, and miraculously we swished along the grass as the glider landed safely on its belly.

I wanted to leap out and kiss the ground, but contented myself with thanking God for my safe return to earth, and for having the experience behind me. Not so. When we reached the dispersal point, I learned to my horror that I was going to have to repeat the performance once a week for a month, alternating between Whitleys and Horsas. Flying was not for me then, and never has been. Since those long-gone days, I have only once taken to the air.

* * *

Back in my Cardiff days, I had managed to replenish my depleted store of lingerie. Quite how Cardiff shops had contrived to maintain such a good supply of pure silk and satin underwear, I did not choose to question. It was sufficient for me to know it was there, and I could buy it. As an officer, I was entitled to a certain amount of leeway in regulation attire, at least that part of it that was concealed from view. On the surface we might all look the same, but underneath—ah, underneath—we were individual, female, and our souls were satin and lace.

One of the bugbears for most officers at Brize Norton was having to take the early morning colour hoisting parade. It took place at the bleary-eyed hour of 6 a.m., hence its unpopularity. Strangely enough, I rather enjoyed getting up early. I had always been an early riser and found it no real hardship. As a consequence, I frequently obliged my fellow officers by taking their "dawn patrol." Although, as I said, I did not mind the hour, it did often mean a bit of a scramble, throwing on clothes and frantically pedalling over to the point where the parade assembled.

The parade itself was a combination of R.A.F. and W.A.A.F. flights, and the raising of the flag was a very serious affair. The R.A.F. officer of the day would shout the commands, and as the flag was slowly hoisted to the top of the pole, we would solemnly salute it. A simple enough procedure one would think, and so it was, but not without its pitfalls. On one occasion, all stiff and starched, I was standing alongside the R.A.F. officers, in front of the parade, when I became aware of a peculiar sensation, an uncomfortable feeling that grew into a certainty. While the flag was going up, my luscious French satin knickers were coming down. Oh no, they can't be, I thought in alarm, but from the stifled laughter coming from behind me, I knew they had. Glancing down, I could see a little mound of blue satin and coffee-coloured lace around my ankles. It transpired that in my hurry to dress, I had failed to secure the little pearl button, and the jolt of my salute had brought the force of gravity into action. I cast about desperately for some graceful way out of this embarrassment, but not too surprisingly no solution presented itself. Oh well, I thought, nonchalant dignity—that's the ticket. The nonchalance did not quite come off, I am afraid, as by now my cheeks were flaming, but with as much dignity as I could muster, I stepped out of the shimmering little pile, and gathering it up, tucked it in front of my tunic and resumed my ceremonial duties.

I braced myself for the inevitable upon entering the Mess at breakfast. The grapevine had been busy, and it was a stop-press item throughout the camp. "Hello Moo, old girl, hear you lost your knickers on parade this morning. Was it colour lowering?" "Hear you were wearing your knockouts today, Moo . . . blue satin, too . . . yum, yum." The gibes went on for days, and there was nothing for it but to laugh along with the rest with as good grace as I could manage.

Unfortunately, the incident was followed all too rapidly by another. I happened to be duty officer the day someone tied a W.A.A.F.'s blackouts onto the flag pole, and they were flying merrily away when we all arrived for the daily ceremonial. They, of course, had to be lowered before the flag could be raised. As the W.A.A.F. officer on duty, I was naturally on the receiving end of both official questions and unofficial hoots of derision. "Goodness, not you again, with another colour hoisting problem." It was little wonder my nickname became "Knickers" for the balance of my posting.

Apart from my seemingly endless battle against rising and falling knickers, there were other fateful problems on my duty roster. I should explain that two of my greatest fears in life at that time were being out in the dark, and rats. As a result, the job I hated most as duty officer was a night tour of the camp. Accompanied by an R.A.F. non-commissioned officer, the W.A.A.F. duty officer had to cover every nook and cranny on the station. Frequently on these excursions, we would come across courting couples in places where they were not supposed to be, and doing things they were certainly not supposed to be doing. It was bad enough having to play spoilsport by moving them on, but the part of the job I hated most of all was inspecting dustbins late at night. The purpose of this was to check that the lids were secure and that there was no litter lying around.

On one particular occasion, I was being accompanied on my rounds by a tiny little R.A.F. sergeant. He could not have been more than about five feet four or five. I know I felt like an Amazon beside him. As we rounded a corner, with only the beam of light from his torch showing us the way, an enormous rat shot out from the back of a dustbin and headed straight for us. From that moment on, rank did not come into my considerations. I gave a piercing shriek and jumped onto the sergeant's back. He, poor chap, did his best to keep me aloft, but staggered under the unexpected weight. Somehow he managed to keep upright, but only just, as the rat ran between his feet. I was far too petrified to jump down, so the poor little man had to piggy-back me to the front of the building. Here, dignity was restored. I climbed down, straightened my uniform, and we continued our inspection. The sergeant and I never talked about this ludicrous adventure, but a bond grew between us, a secret and rather special bond that continued throughout our time of working together.

Despite the foregoing, there were peaceful moments at Brize Norton, and some very pleasant diversions. One of these was Sunday tea at the Priory in Burford. The Priory was the home of the Southby family, who had extended a standing invitation to the officers at our station to come on Sundays whenever they could. I loved going for the pleasure it gave me to slip, for a little while, into an Edwardian time warp. It was a beautiful house with a magnificent garden. The lawns were velvet, and we used to sit under a vast mulberry tree while Darjeeling tea was poured and cucumber sandwiches of tissue paper thinness were passed around. Lady Bracknell would have adored the Priory.

The family were delightful, and Commander Southby had a particularly distinguished career. It is rather ironic that as a military man he had survived the dangers of at least two wars, but that it was his final post-war duty that killed him. He had been appointed one of the official observers at Belsen, and while there contracted some particularly lethal virus and died shortly after.

I went back to see the Priory a few years ago and rather wished I hadn't. I longed to find myself, like a character in a play, in a flashback sequence to a time of golden summers and leisurely teas on the lawn. Instead, the shadows had lengthened. Nothing I had known could be seen anywhere, and I could hear no remembered voices in my head.

Out of the Blue

O NE DAY when I returned from duty, there was a letter
waiting for me with unfamiliar writing on the envelope. Who can this be from, I thought, as I opened it and
started to read. The more I read, the more interested I
became. The letter was from an R.A.F. fighter pilot called
George Pushman. The name rang a distant bell, which
gradually became less distant as I got further into the letter. Of course, I remembered, he is the George Pushman
we were all supposed to look out for back in 1939. He had
written to us almost four years ago, saying he had arrived
in England, had been given our address and told to contact us. It seemed he was the nephew of my aunt's friend
in Ottawa, and as I recalled we had been thoroughly
alerted as to his presence in England. My aunt had written
that he was coming; George had written that he had come;
I had written back about his coming to visit; and then
nobody had written another word—until now. I settled
back into my chair and started to read the letter once more
from the beginning, now that I had sorted out exactly who
it was who was writing to me.

He began by apologizing for not having come to make
himself known to us in 1939, but he had been stationed in
Scotland, which I had to admit was a long way from Guildford. Then when war broke out, he had joined a night
fighter squadron and had been on almost constant duty
during the Battle of Britain. After that, the letter continued, he had returned to Canada to do an advanced naviga-
tion course and, he added rather ruefully, to receive an

147

almighty rocket from his aunt for not having made contact with us. This is some letter, I thought, as I snuggled deeper into my chair, there are pages of it. He was, he said, stationed at present near Bath, and he had casually mentioned in the Mess one evening that he had to try to track down a girl who had become an officer in the W.A.A.F. and what a job it was going to be. Where did he begin? I could tell you where to begin, you ninny, I thought—namely with the original address you had—but then as I read on, I realized that this logic would just have spoiled a good story. He went on to relate that the W.A.A.F. to whom he was telling the tale of his proposed search asked what the girl's name was, and when he told her she burst out laughing. She went on to explain that she knew the said girl very well and could tell him exactly where to find her. So here he was, he concluded, really anxious to meet and make amends for past inadequacies. He did not know how I would feel about the idea, but could we meet, perhaps in Oxford, for dinner? He gave me his address and telephone number, and signed off apologetically mine.

Well—out of the blue—I thought. I found the whole prospect rather amusing, and could not wait for Ruth to come in so that I could tell her. I had liked the letter, and felt the beginning of an interest in the elusive George Pushman. Yes, I thought firmly, I would like to have dinner with you, George Pushman. So I replied to his letter, not at once I must add; there was no need to let him think I was too eager. Besides, had I not had to wait nearly four years before he got around to writing to me?

As it happened, I got bogged down with work anyway. I had four Wings for Victory Parades to prepare for—Oxford, Swindon, Cirencester, and Witney. The preparation involved my visiting each of these towns to check on the routes to be marched and to inspect the churches to find out where the W.A.A.F. were to sit, as well as the actual organization of our part of the parade.

I remember our first parade was in Witney. It was a clear bright day, but with a stiffish wind blowing. The command was given, and one by one the flights began to move forward, marching in time to the band playing nearest to their flight, ours being the band of the Salvation Army. My balloon operators— now trainee flight mechanics— were in perfect unison, marching with the precision of a Guards Regiment. I had promised them we would be something to be proud of, and we were.

After the church service was finished, we re-formed to march back. Once again, we fell in behind the Salvation Army, with me at the head of my flight. Just in front of me, a little bandsman was blowing enthusiastically on the most enormous and elaborate instrument. It was a thing of huge, endless coils, terminating in a monstrous open trumpet head. I could see the effort he was putting into it, and after a while I could also see that he was having trouble with a terrible build-up of saliva. Every time he tipped his instrument to empty it, the strong wind shot it straight back in my direction. By the end of the parade, I was absolutely drenched and not a pretty sight.

On another occasion, we had a Wings for Victory garden fete on the station, and there was wild excitement when Clark Gable, who was stationed nearby, gave us his first aid kit to raffle. It fetched twenty-five pounds, which was a king's ransom in those days.

Between all these ceremonials and my other duties, I had not really given much thought to George Pushman, but looking at my calendar I saw that the time arranged for our dinner date was this coming Saturday. George had suggested the Mitre, a lovely old hotel in Oxford, and wrote that he had booked a table for seven o'clock.

I was rather looking forward to this date, but even more so to going to Oxford, where at that point I had not been since attending a May Ball in 1938 at Magdalen College. Despite the fact that five years of time and tragedy separated me from my seventeen-year-old self, Oxford was still synonymous in my mind with capitalized Romance. I remembered how after the ball we had walked along the banks of the river in the early hours of the morning, the branches of the young green willows touching the water, a college man at my side, and I had wondered if life could possibly hold anything more splendid than this.

Well, we shall see what Oxford has to offer this time, I thought, as I cycled to the small country railway station near Brize Norton, called Bampton. I boarded the "Bampton Flier," a self-important little train with a jaunty steam engine the colour of unripe apples. There was always a lot of bustle about the Flier's take-offs, much shunting and grunting, toot-toots of whistles, and finally a billowing puff of steam as away it went.

I had decided to spend the whole day in Oxford, exploring and doing precisely what I felt like doing. I bought a picnic lunch and wandered down to the banks of the Isis. It was beautifully still; the only sound was the singing of the larks high above me. I trailed my hand in the water and fed the eager ducks who came at the rustle of paper from my lunch bag. I leant back, the summer sun on my face, and for the first time in months felt at peace with myself.

By the time seven o'clock came, I had had such a lovely day, I did not really care if I ever met George Pushman. As I went through the door of the Mitre, I began to wonder if I would be able to pick him out, or if he would be able to identify me. The place was crowded, and I had just started to scan the faces in the foyer when I felt a touch on my arm, and turned.

A tall man in Air Force uniform was standing beside me, with a smile that lit up the room. It was impossible to feel formal, ill at ease, or distant with such a smile. Although we introduced ourselves with the ordinary pleasantries, I had the oddest feeling that something quite out of the ordinary had happened. I could not really define it, but it was rather how I had felt once when I was lost as a child and then had found my way home.

We spent the evening getting to know each other. I told him about my family and my home. He, in turn, told me about his people in Ottawa and about my aunt in Canada.

He explained how he had decided to come to England to learn to fly, never drea╨.ing that a war would be declared eight months after his arrival. He obviously loved England, and we talked about places we had been to and things we had done. We talked with the ease of old friends, and I could not believe it when I looked at my watch and realized that I had only ten minutes to get to the railway station for the last train back to camp.

I thought about George all the way back to Brize Norton. He was unlike anyone I had ever met before. Despite everything he had been through as a fighter pilot, life for him was wonderful. His sheer delight in it, his tremendous vitality, and his complete lack of pretension seemed like a fresh wind blowing through a stuffy room. I brought his voice back to mind, and thought again what an attractive accent he had. For someone who had gone off on this date more in a spirit of curiosity than anything else, I reflected, I seem to be spending a lot of time re-shooting the scene.

I began to see a lot of George in the next few weeks. He had the great advantage of having the use of a small airplane to get himself around, and he would think nothing of flying up to Brize Norton to have dinner with me in the Mess. This, as you can imagine, evoked the usual arch glances, pointed questions, and huddled confabs. I did not have anything to tell them. It was all I could do to keep up with George's accelerated pace. I felt as though I were trying to stay abreast of a decathlon man. Barely would I catch my breath from the sprint, so to speak, before he was off over the hurdles, bounding into the long jump, and vaulting over the bar. Twenty-four hours in his day were simply not enough to take in all the things that delighted him.

I had forty-eight hours' leave coming to me and decided to ask George if he would like to come home with me. He leapt at the invitation, and I telephoned my parents to prepare for yet another guest. On these occasions, my mother would surpass herself. We none of us questioned too deeply exactly how she conjured up the remarkable wartime meals that she did. We all suspected that she had the art of bartering down to a fine science. My father, the soul of probity, had stipulated from the beginning that there would be no dealings with the black market in his family. What we could not get legitimately, we would have to learn to do without. My mother said, "Of course, Irving, what an idea," and set off on her rounds. She would pack up her shopping basket with the produce from the farm— a couple of chickens, lots of lovely brown eggs, fruit in season, and perhaps some of her carefully-grown asparagus, tender beans, and peas—and away she would toddle to Guildford, returning some hours later with all manner of rationed goods. My father seemed totally unaware of anything untoward, and the rest of us wisely asked no questions.

I met George in London and we travelled home together. When he asked me if he could bring his dog, I knew then that he would fit in, but I still tried to prepare him for some of the eccentricities of life at the farm. Diana was home from school and waiting for us at the gate with a retinue of Warren Farm House dogs beside her. There was a mad scene as George's dog was greeted, at first with suspicion and much growling and flying of fur, and finally with the respect due a lady. Eventually they all took off amicably enough to show her around their territory.

The rest of the family were awaiting our arrival with ill-concealed curiosity. We were greeted, as was befitting, in the front hall, but after a while it seemed natural that we should all drift into the kitchen. I think the kitchen was my favourite room in the whole house. There was a large boiler in the corner, belting out heat even in mid-summer. The walls were incredibly old, and the ceiling low and beamed.

As we went in, I was a little embarrassed to see a cat curled up in the centre of the old pine table. She was shooed away towards her new litter of kittens, who were mewing from their nursery in the cupboard. Meanwhile, Nellie's budgies were vying loudly for attention, and it seemed to me the scene was set for the Mad Hatter's tea party. I glanced at George and was relieved to see he was totally unperturbed. He was, and is, one of those fortunate people who have the knack of fitting into any surroundings with unselfconscious ease. The old brown teapot was brought out, and we all sat around drinking tea and telling George (all at once, I might add) about the farm. After a while, my father gave George the nod, indicating that tea was all right but there were better beverages to be had. The two of them shambled off in the direction of the old dairy, now the family air raid shelter, to draw themselves a pint of the best from the bottomless wooden barrel we always kept there.

In the next couple of days, George had captivated my parents, won Diana forever, and made a slave of Nellie, who giggled at his outrageous jokes and then slipped him an extra rasher of bacon or a second egg. Forty-eight hours is little more than a wink in time, but it was long enough for George to find out that he was as attracted to us as a family as we were to him.

As we travelled back on the train together to London, he asked me to marry him. I had half expected it, but was still surprised to hear myself saying yes without any hesitation or demurring. All the doubts, the self-examination, the qualms that had held me back from commitments before, simply did not seem to exist. It was as though everything else in my life had been for the purpose of matching me with this man at this moment.

Something Borrowed, Something Blue

W E CHOSE the fourteenth of August for our wedding
day, just a little more than six weeks away. It did not
give us much time, but my father was in his element and
undertook to mastermind the whole affair.

Transportation being what it was, he said we would
have to have some place central. We chose London's oldest
church, St. Bartholomew-the-Great. It is a gorgeous
church, next door to the hospital, both of which were
founded by Henry I's court jester in 1123, and I was
thrilled at the thought of being married there. It made me
feel somehow that I was part of England's history. The
Butchers' Guild, one of the City's ancient livery compa-
nies, had their hall nearby in St. Bartholomew's Close,
and my father arranged to book it for the reception. When
George found out where we were holding the reception, he
said he would love to be a fly on the wall when relatives in
Canada opened their mail and saw "Butchers' Hall" on an
engraved invitation. He said he could just see them wondering "whatever has George got himself into" as they pictured a bride picking her way genteelly over a sawdust-
strewn floor, with great slabs of meat hanging from the
ceiling. As it turned out, we got in just in time, as only a
few months later the Butchers' Hall was badly damaged in
an air raid, and it was not until the 1960s that it was re-
built.

Most of the arrangements were finalized over the telephone—in a triangular manner. My father would telephone me and then I would telephone George, who would

then telephone my father. Luckily George was able to get home more often than I, so he was able to do a good deal of the planning. He slipped so naturally into the family that it seemed there had never been a time when George was not part of the life at Warren Farm House.

My main task, on my next leave pass, was to meet up with my mother in London to shop for my trousseau, and most important of all, my wedding dress. I gather from today's young that trousseaus are definitely passé, but it was a vital part of the prenuptial rites to my generation.

A year or so ago, I chanced upon a honeymoon couple at a hotel, where they arrived on their wedding night, unencumbered by any apparent luggage. She wore jeans and carried all she needed— presumably a toothbrush and the pill— in her shoulder bag. She did not know what she was missing. I can remember so vividly the wonderful Christmassy feeling of collecting my trousseau, and the fun my mother and I had doing it.

We had arranged to meet at Harrod's, and my mother arrived at our rendez-vous point, armed to the teeth with clothing coupons. Many of these had been given to her by the Canadian servicemen who passed through our house. It was a heady feeling to know there were no restrictions for once, and we headed straight for the lingerie department. We emerged hours later with three filmy nightgowns, a French satin dressing gown in bands of palest marshmallow pink and green, and a supply of gossamer silk camiknickers.

We checked out the bridal shop at Harrod's but did not see anything that either of us really liked, so we moved along in the direction of Oxford Street. After several unsuccessful forays into several shops, we went into the bridal department at Bourne and Hollingsworth, and there it was— a dress to take one's breath away. I knew I just had to have it. It seemed to float like a cloud on a summer's day. Demurely Victorian in style and fashioned in delicate muslin, the full skirt was gathered in frilled tiers and fell from an empire bodice, with a high neck and leg-of-mutton sleeves. The veil flowed down from the headdress of silk forget-me-nots into a long train, and continued the Victorian theme with a double-frill edging. My mother and I looked at each other. Would it be too big, too small, too something? It was not anything but perfect! When I came out to look at it in the light, the other shoppers clapped their approval, and the dress of my dreams was mine.

We shopped for the rest of the day, buying cotton dresses, a lovely crepe "going away" dress, and a wickedly chic little navy blue suit. These all had to be matched up with shoes, hats, gloves— did we really wear gloves?— and handbags. At the end of the day, my father joined us, and for the last time as Muriel Gane, I had dinner with my parents in London. We said goodnight and I hugged them both, not just in thanks for the lovely clothes they had bought to see me properly launched, but for a lifetime of love.

I arrived back at the base to find out that I had been promoted to Acting Flight Officer. Any other time, I would have been over the moon, but so much was happening all at once that I could not quite take it all in.

Liz was to be married on Saturday, and as no one had coupons to squander on bridesmaids' finery, it had been agreed I should wear one of my evening dresses. I dug up a peach taffeta I had had before the war. Together with matching peach satin shoes and some peach roses in my hair, I managed to co-ordinate relatively well into the wedding tableau. Liz looked beautiful and radiant— as every bride should. Her tall American groom beamed, and looked as though he had just obtained a jewel beyond price— as every groom should. They left for their honeymoon in Bournemouth, and for a moment I felt a twinge of sadness when I remembered my grandmother and our memorable holiday there.

With Liz's wedding over, I had time to concentrate on my own. My bridesmaids were to be my two sisters, Audrey and Diana. Having left the bulk of our clothing coupons in Bond Street and Knightsbridge, it was fortunate that my mother remembered the two very pretty dresses that Audrey, aged nine, and I, at fourteen, had worn as brides-maids at a posh, pre-war wedding. Audrey, it was decided, would wear my dress, and Diana, now nine, would wear Audrey's. The family seemed to have a passion for peach taffeta, as these dresses were the same colour as the one I had just worn to Liz's wedding. As it turned out, they could have been made to go with my dress. They had full long skirts, with six rows of ruching around the edge. The little boleros were trimmed with the same ruching, and matching net was fluted around the short sleeves. Diana was entranced with herself and could barely be persuaded to take the dress off after she had tried it on.

While preparations were at their height, and everyone was tearing around in all directions, Donald came home. I was on duty at Brize Norton, but Donald called upon my mother, and she had to tell him about my forthcoming marriage. As soon as I heard he was at home, I wrote him the long letter that I had composed in my mind all those months ago. I felt I had let him down, and yet I was so happy and so sure of the rightness of my future with George that I could not dwell on the effects the letter might have on him. At least he was at home now, and it seemed to me that it would be easier to receive a "Dear John" sur-rounded by family than alone somewhere in the desert. I said in my letter that I would like to see him, and a few days later he showed up in the Mess. He took me out to dine in Burford, and over dinner we talked the whole thing out. He said he realized that it had been too much to ex-pect a relationship to endure such time and distance, and that it was at least partly his fault for letting the situation drift, without either clarification or commitment.

I looked at him hopefully. "Please, Don, can we always be friends?"

He took my hands in his and smiled. "Yes, of course, always." We both knew we were saying good-bye—not to each other as people, for we stayed friends for years—but to the boy and girl we had been, and to the glorious, foolish, romantic dreams of adolescence.

The parties in the Mess lasted for well over a week. The officers gave me a large silver cigarette box, engraved "Presented to Section Officer Muriel Gane, with best wishes from the Members of the Officers' Mess at the Royal Air Force Station, Brize Norton, Oxfordshire, on the occasion of her marriage to Flight Lieutenant George R. Pushman, 14th August, 1943." I have it still.

Two of the girls in my flight lived in Northern Ireland, and when they came back from leave, they proudly presented me with a wedding present of six pairs of pure silk stockings. It was a fantastic, sacrificial present, for silk stockings had not been seen in England since the war began.

All "my girls" were as excited as I was, and everybody wanted to come to the wedding. I took the N.C.O.'s aside and told them how much I wanted as many as possible to be there. I invited them to form a Guard of Honour and left the final choice of girls to them.

On the day before the wedding, I made the rounds to say good-bye before I left for home. There was a family dinner arranged for Friday evening at the farm, and the excitement was high. The plan was for my mother and me to catch an early train next morning to take us to London. I would have my hair done while my mother would collect the dress and veil and take them along to the Butchers' Hall. My father had arranged rooms for us to change in, and had ordered us a light snack.

By the time I arrived at the Butchers' Hall, the family had gathered. It seemed to me that Nellie and Flo were very flushed and giggly, and I suspected they had already been at the sherry. Somehow I found myself applying make-up for Nellie and Flo, and fixing Audrey's headdress, and doing everything but getting myself dressed. It was just as well, I suppose, that I was busy or I would have wound myself up into a titanic flap.

Diana was already in a high state of nerves, and she could be impossible in these circumstances. On the way to the church, I was told later, she quite suddenly said to my mother that she was not going, and proceeded to hurl her bouquet on the pavement. Happily my mother, as she always did, rose to the occasion. "Very well, stay here then. Muriel would not want a grumpy-looking bridesmaid in any case." There was a moment of hesitation after which Diana, knowing my mother usually meant what she said, picked up her bouquet and jumped into the waiting Daimler to be borne off to the church.

Finally, there was just my father and I left. He looked at me with tears in his eyes, saying the things that all fathers say on such occasions— how proud he was of me and how lovely I looked, and how he wished only for my complete happiness. With that he kissed me, and we went off together, he holding my hand.

The church was crowded. I was very nervous as I walked up the aisle. I could see, out of the corner of my eye, almost the entire contingent of girls on the flight mechanics course. For a moment, I almost broke into a military stride. It seemed miles to the altar, but finally I was standing beside George. We looked at each other and the ceremony began. I was still nervous, but from the moment we exchanged our vows, the butterflies departed, my pulse stopped racing, and for the first time that day, I felt truly happy.

When we went into the vestry to sign the register, I met the best man for the first time. He was a Colonel Colin Gray, of the Queen's Regiment, and a close friend of George's. He was a charming man, but a soldier after all, and took his duties very seriously. He started to organize us all for the procession back into the church and down the aisle, showing the same attention to detail that he would have done had he been stage-managing the Trooping the Colour. He turned to Diana, who, still wound up, was being difficult again. "Now, Diana," he said, "I would like you to walk behind your sister, Muriel, and Audrey and I will walk together behind you."

Diana's reply was sharp and emphatic. "I certainly will not," she declared, her eyes flashing. This shook the Colonel to his socks. Nobody, but nobody, had ever disobeyed one of his orders, and certainly not a nine-year-old female.

He managed to restrain himself and asked in a controlled voice, "Whyever not, Diana?" looking down at her from his great height.

The horrible child was not even remotely intimidated. Glaring at him, she replied "Well, I don't know you, do I, and how do I know that you won't kick me?"

I am sure that with the thought once implanted, the temptation must have been overwhelming. However, such an act would have been totally at odds with so elegant an officer and a gentleman, and he made no reply, but firmly placed her in the assigned position.

By the time we were out of the church, I could have throttled her myself, and would gladly have done so were it not for the fact that brides traditionally do not go around throttling their little sisters. All the way down the aisle, she kept turning around to glare at the Colonel, and each time she did, she stepped on my wedding veil, which gave me the most almighty jerk. Each time this happened, the procession would grind to a halt until she took her foot off my veil. It was only through the grace of God, and a remarkably firm hair pin, that the veil stayed on my head.

As we emerged from the church and the hazards of the march down the aisle, we passed between our W.A.A.F. Guard of Honour, and I felt very proud and touched by their presence. As we approached the lychgate, my superstitious self was relieved to see the proverbial chimney sweep standing there, as well as an able-bodied young sailor. It was a fair omen, and I made sure that I touched them both in the traditional gesture of good luck. There was also a little crowd of London cockneys clustered around the timbered gate, all wishing "dearie" well, and I waved cheerily at them all.

I doubt if any bridal couple really remembers much in

detail about their wedding reception. I just recall how happy I felt, and how happy everybody else seemed. A great many friends and relatives had made an enormous effort to come, and I was only sorry that George could not have his family there. A surprising number of W.A.A.F. officers from his station near Bath showed up, though, which did his morale no end of good.

I suppose every wartime wedding has a story connected with it, and ours was no exception. George was terribly disappointed when he learned that none of his squadron would be able to attend the wedding, as they had been called out on a special raid. It was the squadron's practice on this type of raid to fly at the lowest possible level. This meant hopping over hedgerows, zooming up over trees and pylons, and trying to reach the target without being detected on the enemy's radar. On this particular raid, they were flying very low and ran into a swarm of locusts, which covered their windscreens like an impenetrable blanket, blocking out all vision ahead. As a result, the planes had to increase their height, and in so doing became targets for the ground defences. It was an ill-fated raid, and tragically quite a number of the squadron were shot down.

One of the men normally on George's crew was among those who bailed out and managed to land in enemy territory. He came down in a field of harvested corn and dived into one of the stooks to hide. The Germans went around the field, thrusting their bayonets into the stooks. Through some unbelievable miracle, they missed out the one in which he was hiding. He stayed hidden in his stook, nursing a broken ankle, until after dark, when he hobbled out and made for cover in some nearby woods.

Interminable hours later, he heard voices but could not distinguish what they were saying, nor in which language they were speaking. If they were Germans, and he called out, the game was up. On the other hand, if they were the Resistance out looking for him, then he would be left in this dark forest, with an ankle desperately needing medical attention. Just then he heard a whistled tune, rationalized that it sounded faintly Gallic, and stumbled out into the clearing. He was in luck. It was the Resistance.

They scurried him off to a farmhouse, hiding him away in the loft. A doctor was brought in to attend to his ankle, and he remained in the loft until he was pronounced fit enough to be moved along the escape route, which took him south over the Pyrenees and into Spain.

The route over the mountains had to be made on foot, and only at night. So it was weeks later that he eventually arrived at the British Embassy in Madrid, to arrange transport home to England. While passing time in the Embassy's waiting room, he was disinterestedly leafing through the pages of a *Tatler* when he stopped, did the classic double take, and stared down at the page in front of him. There was a picture of his friend, brother-in-arms, and boon companion, George Pushman, with his bride, the former Muriel Gane, leaving St. Bartholomew's Church after their wedding. A wedding which he had regrettably been unable to attend.

"A few things held me up," he told us later, "but I feel I sort of got there—one way or another."

A New Life

I WAS NOW a married lady, but the fact did not really sink in until we registered as Mr. and Mrs. George Pushman at the Dorchester, where we were staying for the night before beginning our honeymoon in Cornwall.

The next day we left for two weeks in the charming coastal village of Lelant. We arrived at a delightfully quaint little hotel overlooking the bay. There were only a handful of guests, and it was not difficult to think of ourselves as being almost "alone at last." The first evening at dinner, however, despite our preoccupation with each other, we were transfixed by a couple at a nearby table. He appeared very flamboyant in both manner and dress, and spoke loudly with a strong American accent. His companion was an absolute stunner and beautifully dressed. Before we knew it, he was over at our table and pressing us to join them. It turned out he was an American living in London. She was an Estonian and a "raff-u-gee" as she explained to us in a rich Baltic accent.

In addition to their elegant wardrobes, they seemed to want for nothing. They had their own Cona coffee-making machine on their table and, he confided to us, he never travelled anywhere without a crate of live chickens. He would entrust these to a local, whom he would notify whenever he took a fancy for chicken—which seemed to be practically every day. He always had cold chicken for elegant picnics on the beach, and when he found out we were on our honeymoon, nothing would do but to have us share his supply.

One of the other necessities to the Good Life that he could not do without, he told us, was a mint julep. He was flabbergasted to learn that not only had I never tasted a mint julep, I had never heard of a mint julep. Such an overwhelming gap in my education had to be remedied, and he invited us up to his room so that I could taste the best mint julep north of Kentucky. I had to agree, it was delicious.

We were having such a heavenly time that we were crushed when George was recalled from leave after only one week. It transpired that our "chicken man" and his gorgeous lady were returning to London on the same day we were leaving, and he kindly invited us to share his taxi to the station. It sounded a good idea so we accepted, only to find that the taxi, capacious and all as it was, was filled to the bursting point with their mountainous supply of luggage. A crate full of the remaining chickens, all cackling loudly, was lashed to the luggage rack on the roof. There was simply not an inch of space for human passengers. In the end, the taxi went on without us and we all had to walk to the station.

The amazing man had, of course, booked a private carriage, and declared that he would be "mighty offended" if we did not join him. The train was at its wartime norm, i.e., packed to overflowing, and we had a terrible time trying to jostle our way through to his reserved carriage. Once there, however, he closed the door and proceeded to get down his traveling bar. Within minutes he had mixed a lavish supply of mint juleps, complete with ice cubes, and we downed these while the crushed and envious masses outside looked thirstily on. I felt horribly embarrassed, as though, like Marie Antoinette, I were munching cake while the starving poor of Paris were denied even a crust of bread. This twinge of social conscience, however, did nothing to diminish my enjoyment of the mint juleps, a beverage to which I was rapidly becoming addicted.

Arriving back home with another week of my honeymoon still to go, and without George, was a very odd feeling. Now, as George's wife, I had to say good-bye as he dashed back to his station. It was I who was left behind, a reverse situation, as always before it had been I who was doing the leaving. In the past, I had never really minded being on my own, but now I felt very lonely and strangely apprehensive. It was a different sort of worry than any I had ever felt before. George was not just part of my life, but part of me. It was a completely new sensation, and I was not all that sure I liked it. I sighed. My carefree days were over.

Happily, however, George was now posted to an R.A.F. station near Camberley, which was only about eighteen miles from Guildford. Consequently, in the last week of my leave, he spent almost as much time with me as he did at the station. Still, it was not the same, and I was glad when my leave was up and I could return to Brize Norton and keep myself busy.

When I arrived back at the station, my welcome was as warm as ever, but a little restraint had crept in. I began to realize why I had always felt rather sorry for married women in the Services. Once the plain little band of gold was placed on the third finger, left hand, a woman was somehow categorized, out of bounds and no longer just answerable to herself. Most of us in this situation, I think, experienced the same contradictory emotions. We were thrilled and happy to be married to the one we had chosen, yet we still wanted to be treated as single, with the old easy camaraderie unchanged. I suppose the truth of the matter was that we were not really mature enough to assume the role of settled married woman, particularly when "settled" was precisely what we were not.

So life continued, as wartime life did, always on the knife's edge. George was off on fighter-bomber sorties several times a day, and was under incredible stress. He did his best not to show it, as he wanted our fleeting times together to be as happy as possible. Yet I knew the extent of the pressures when they would find an escape hatch in nightmares. At that time George was flying with a French squadron, whose crew were inexperienced and not performing to his exacting standards. I would wake from sleep some nights to hear George shouting indignantly, with a very colourful range of expletives to "get in tight . . . get in lower" and further instructions on what they could do with their excuses. This would be followed by a lot of tossing and turning and finally the dead sleep of exhaustion.

I would have liked to know when he was on "ops," so that mentally I could have been with him. This, of course, was impossible, and so there I was, half myself flying with George and the other half trying to do my job, with my heart not really in it anymore.

Midnight Ride

EVERYTHING was to change six weeks later, when I discovered that I was pregnant. Expectant mums were not catered to in the W.A.A.F. Somehow the uniform and a bun in the oven were not compatible, and I knew my days in the Air Force were numbered— a month or so at the most.

While I felt excited by the news, the thought of being a mother awed me. I had not really become used to being a wife yet. Now, in a little while, I would be at home in a daughter's role again, and at the same time preparing to be a mother. The thought of this consequence of marriage had seemed so remote in the all-too-recent romantic days of our courtship. If I had let it cross my mind at all, it was a vision of us settled into a charming house of our own, with a pretty nursery and a plain nanny. Instead, here I was, with George off in the wild blue yonder, and my own career facing a certain end. I became depressed with the thought of becoming a pregnant widow. Then what? Being a widow would be bad enough, but a pregnant widow? I shuddered at the thought and was ashamed that I should allow myself even to think of such a situation.

In addition to all these un-maternal thoughts, I had started to suffer from morning sickness, to say nothing of mid-day sickness, twilight sickness, and bedtime sickness. I dreaded having to go out and take a parade, for I never seemed to have any warning of an attack of nausea. I could understand now why Victorian ladies took to their bed with the vapours. I found all I wanted to do was to lie down like some wild little animal, curl up into a ball, and die. Yet, conversely, I did not want to reveal my secret to anyone. For as long as I could, I wanted to stay me, Acting Flight Officer Pushman, and not a ballooning mum-to-be.

Eventually, I felt I had to tell my mother. I will always remember her face when I broke the news. Was I absolutely sure? How was I feeling? What did George think? This barrage of questions, I felt, was buying her time to recover from the shock. Although she did not say so, I sensed that she felt having a baby now was unwise with the precarious sort of life George was leading. I could not have agreed with her more, but then in those pre-pill days, what did wisdom have to do with it? However, Mother, as she always did, collected herself and said the right things. It was wonderful news, and how thrilled she would be to be a grandmother, and how marvellous for me to become a mother now, so I would be able to enjoy my children while I was still young. We hugged each other to celebrate our shared secret, and slowly I began to feel better about it all, and even rather excited.

Nothing stayed a secret very long in our family. Soon everybody knew. Audrey was a bit guarded, but Diana revelled in the idea of becoming an aunt at the tender age of nine. My parents insisted on my coming home to stay when I left the W.A.A.F. in November. George and I could have the self-contained flat that had been my grandmother's, at the far end of the house. It was all settled.

Back at Brize Norton I had time to re-assess the change my fortunes had taken. When you are caught up in one particular phase of your life, you feel it will go on forever, the wheels happily turning, and you feel oddly at a loss when everything stops and suddenly veers off in another direction.

I felt this way now that I was about to leave the W.A.A.F. I could not go back and pick up the kind of life I had had before the war. The person I was now had nothing in common with the shy, uncertain teen-ager who had tearfully waved good-bye at Guildford station on a snowy January morning almost three years ago.

Strangely enough, it helped to know that although I was leaving Brize Norton, so, too, were all my newly-trained flight mechanics. Our era there was coming to a joint end. I was starting a new life, and they were about to be dispersed to continue the job for which they had been trained. It now seemed a more natural separation, as we were all simply part of a unit that was breaking up.

They knew that they were going, but they did not know that I was. I decided to call them together one day and tell them, so that they would be the first ones on the base to hear. I was thinking about this as I caught the last train back to Bampton after a brief reunion with George. It was the train Ruth usually caught, and I hoped to meet up with her so that we could cycle back together.

For some reason, she was not on the train, and I was forced to face my old phobia of being alone in the dark. The thought of cycling back on my own was nightmarish. It involved going around the perimeter track—almost three miles—along a course that followed an ill-lit and lonely road bordered by heavy woodland. In my mind, I saw the darting shadows and the skeletal trees, and heard in my imagination the bicycle wheels crunching on the stony path, the soughing of the wind, and the sound of my own heart beating. It was too much.

The only other choice, however, was to leave the station and cross the runways to the camp on the other side, only half a mile away. This latter course was only permitted if there was no night flying in progress. If there was night flying, then a flag was flown to warn people away from the runways. I left the railway station and looked across towards the flagpole. It was a very dark winter's night and to my relief I saw no flag, so I set off at a cracking pace across the airfield. I crossed the first runway. Thank God that is behind me, I thought, when to my unspeakable horror, I heard the sudden roar of aircraft engines, getting louder with every passing second. I became frenzied with panic. Which way should I go . . . forwards? . . . backwards? Either way I felt I was about to be killed, and nobody would know until my mangled remains were found the following day. Poor George, poor unborn baby, I thought wildly. The only cool thought that penetrated my frantic brain was that if the aircraft kept to the runways, all might yet be well. At that moment, I was in between the two. If, on the other hand, they used the whole airfield as they sometimes did, there was no escape. Better not think about it, I sobbed inwardly, and threw myself down on the grass, covering myself with my bicycle.

It was a pretty futile sort of protection, admittedly, but it gave me the illusion of cover. I pressed my hands over my ears, closed my eyes tightly, and prayed as I had never prayed before. I did not dare move. Even with my blocked ears, the noise was deafening and the ground beneath me was shuddering as though being torn by an earthquake. Then, quite suddenly, all was quiet. I felt myself all over. I was still alive, and through a miracle, unhurt. I was crying—out of panic, fear, relief, and a wild joy at still being among the quick and not the dead. I gathered myself together, picked up my bicycle, and streaked towards the other runway. I could not be sure that another squadron was not about to take off, but across that runway lay sanctuary. There was no other way, and I know I could have won the Tour de France the way I pedalled across the tarmac to the other side.

What I had done was a serious offence in the eyes of the R.A.F., so the quicker I could slink home and slip into bed, the better. As I undressed, I was still shaking violently, and gradually became aware that a new and different fear was creeping into my mind. Would this night's adventure affect my unborn child?

I recalled old wives' tales of women being frightened by mice, and having their babies born with little rodents on their tiny foreheads. Heaven forbid that my baby enter this world with a Whitley bomber or a Horsa glider stamped on his— or her— brow. Too awful to contemplate, and my shivering started all over again. I must never, ever, tell anyone, I thought, but must trust in a kindly God to spare my child the sins of its mother and the mark of my midnight ride.

Bright Future

EACH DAY that passed brought me nearer to the day of my discharge. I should have been happy, but inexplicably I was sad, not just at the thought of leaving my friends but also at leaving behind this part of my life. While I would be safe and comfortable in the bosom of the family, I would not have any Air Force friends to gossip with, and no husband around to fuss over me.

George's flying duties were increasing all the time, and when he was not up in the air, he would be back in the Mess—a Mess just like the one I was leaving. He would be having a whale of a time—I knew all about life in a Mess—and where would I be? I would be chewing digestive tablets, or munching on dry biscuits, or worse still, in the bathroom with my head in the wash basin. I wondered if I were unique, or if other women in my situation felt the same conflicting emotions.

I was to be given a big send-off in the Mess on the night prior to my departure. That day I took down my photographs and packed them into my suitcase with a heavy heart. By this time tomorrow, there would be a new W.A.A.F. officer in my room. I went on morosely, emptying my drawers, and making two neat littles piles on my bed—W.A.A.F. issue to be returned to Stores in one, and my own private bits and pieces in the other. The big house was so still, and so silent, for everyone was out and about, getting on with their duties, while I was here alone with no duties to carry out.

I cannot go on like this, I told myself, so I left my packing

and went out in search of some company. I walked to the
far side of the camp in the direction of the W.A.A.F.'s billet
and saw a crowd coming towards me. They had come to
collect me and take me back with them for a special little
farewell. They presented me with small, touching good-bye
presents; we exchanged addresses and promises to "keep
in touch." I heard about their new postings and wished
them luck, and gave each of them, as my farewell gift, pictures of the Guard of Honour at our wedding.

We did not keep in touch, we never met again, and we
never wrote. Yet as I think about it now, perhaps we did
not need to. We were locked in each other's personal histo-
ries for all time. We belong together in a special part of our
lives, and I, for one, think perhaps that I prefer to remember friends as they were— as we all were— young and full of
promise.

The Mess party was a happy affair, but already I felt that
I no longer belonged. The show would go on and tomorrow
someone else would walk into the mess, conversations
would stop, and she would be assessed, measured, and
accepted, as I had been. My name would be replaced by
hers, and in a little while I would be forgotten. Yesterday's
news, I thought forlornly.

I decided not to go to Mess for breakfast. I wanted to
leave with the memories of the party, and the laughter,
and the good times. I could not face any more farewells,
and besides, I felt as sick as a dog. I gathered up my uniforms and looked at them lovingly. I had been so proud of
them, but now they were getting ever so slightly tight at
the seams. I had sold them to a pretty young W.A.A.F. officer who would at least do justice to them, I comforted
myself.

It felt like the final day of the final term at school as I
folded these symbols of another life neatly on my bed and
began dressing in my unfamiliar civilian clothes. I turned
to look in the full mirror, and what I saw made it hard for
me to believe that I had ever worn the uniform of the
Women's Auxiliary Air Force.

I sighed, and with a shrug of my shoulders left the W.A.A.F. as I had entered it— lonely, a little depressed, and more than a bit apprehensive about what lay ahead. I walked past the guardroom, tears rolling down my cheeks, and out into the bright morning of my future.

THE END

c